BICYCLE

The Noblest Invention

BICYCLE

The Noblest Invention

FOREWORD BY LANCE ARMSTRONG

RODALE

This edition first published in the UK in 2003 by
Rodale Ltd
7–10 Chandos Street
London W1G 9AD

www.rodale.co.uk

Photograph and illustration credits are listed on page 313.

Consultants for UK and Australian editions: Sgt Nigel Tottie, North Yorkshire Police; Senior
Constable Mick Shaw, Northern Territory Police; Nick Heywood and Gerard Thomas, 26inches.com;
John Middleton of the British Cycling Museum; John Kitchiner, *Mountain Bike Rider* magazine; Patrick Adams.

Book design by
studio **cactus** Ⓒ

A CIP record for this book is available from the British Library

ISBN 1–4050–3430–0

Distributed to the book trade by Pan Macmillan Ltd

1 3 5 7 9 8 6 4 2

Notice

Visit us on the web at *www.bicycling.com*

WE **INSPIRE** AND **ENABLE** PEOPLE TO IMPROVE
THEIR LIVES AND THE WORLD AROUND THEM

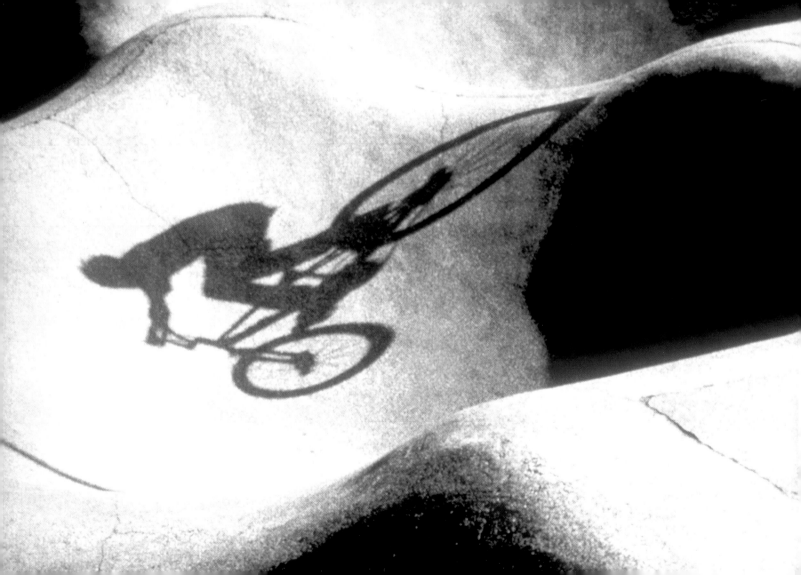

CONTENTS

FOREWORD

By Lance Armstrong

A bicycle is the long sought-after means of transportation for all of us who have runaway hearts. Our first bike is a matter of kerb-jumping, puddle-splashing liberation; it's freedom from supervision, from car pools and from curfews. It's a merciful release from parental reliance – one's own way to the movies or a friend's house. More plainly, it's the first chance we have to choose our own direction.

A bike is the first wheeled machine we ever steer solely by ourselves, and, perhaps for that reason, we have intense affection for and strangely specific memories of the ones we've owned. I myself have had hundreds of them, but they stay with me, like old friends. The physical familiarity you gain with a bike is something you don't feel for any other vehicle, no matter how sweet the ride. My own first bike was a Schwinn Mag Scrambler that I got when I was about seven. It was an ugly brown and yellow contraption, but it was the start of my lifelong attachment to bikes, an attachment that has acquired physical proportions: there are times when I swear a bike is merely an extension of my arms and legs. All these years later, I still have a faint sensation of that first Schwinn, how the rubber handgrips moulded to my palms and how the soles of my trainers grabbed the teeth of the pedals.

My mother, Linda, still has most of the bike parts I've ever owned. The once-shiny components are boxed up and put away; she can't bear to toss them out because they were so hard to come by. When I was a boy, she worked as a secretary, and it was an expensive proposition for her to buy a bike and all the racing parts I wanted. We lived in an apartment in the suburbs of Dallas, across the street from a shop called the Richardson Bike Mart. The owner, a guy named Jim Hoyt, had turned it into the headquarters for cycling in the area. Jim knew us from the neighbourhood, and he noticed how hard my mother worked and that I was always neat and well behaved. He helped my mother pick out my bikes and gave her deals on them. From then on, the Richardson Bike Mart was where I bought every bike and part I owned over the next decade. That store formed me as a cyclist. I would wander through it staring at the latest gears. I always had a thing for newness, for the latest technology that might result in the smallest increment of speed.

Of course, it's the fastest bikes you remember best. I circled old dirt tracks at Richardson's on a BMX bike. I ran neighbourhood traffic lights on my first good 10-speed, a beautiful blue Mercier, slim and elegant, that I got when I was 13. Next, I had a top-of-the-line Raleigh with real racing wheels, but I only owned it a short time before I got into a crash by running an amber light. I used to like to ride in traffic for the challenge, and one afternoon I whirled through a busy junction when out of nowhere came a Ford Bronco that hit me straight on. I went flying headfirst through the junction while metal parts from the totalled bike sprayed all around me.

The last bike of my boyhood was a Schwinn Paramount, which I rode along the black-ribbon rural roads of Texas, dodging pickup trucks as I went for miles through fields as brown as coffee. That Schwinn took me all the way to Moscow – my first trip overseas – for the Junior World Championships. Aboard my current Trek, a fabulous machine of composites so light I can lift it with one hand, I've explored all the different pavements of Europe. I've ridden the bone-jarring and cobblestone-studded coastal roads along the north Atlantic, the winding black-grey routes of the Alps, and the parched and jagged approaches to the Pyrenees.

I've been asked many times what keeps me on my bike. How do I explain my desire to ride for hours and even days at a time, up and over mountainsides? The Tour de France is arguably the most gruelling sporting event on the face of the earth: we pedal around the circumference of an entire country, over a period of three weeks in wind, rain and scorching sun, across Alps, through flats, along coastlines, past graveyards and lavender fields, over cobblestones and slick pavement. Why do I do it? The simple answer is that I love to ride. I ride out of season as passionately as I ride in season. One afternoon I was out on my bike when my mobile rang. It was David Millar, the great young British cyclist and my friend, calling from Paris. He was out on the town and had a few drinks and decided to give me a ring.

'Please tell me you're not on your bike,' he said.

'I'm on my bike.'

'No! You bastard! It's December bloody first! How long have you been on it?'

'Three and a half hours.'

'No!'

To me, riding is living. When I was sick with cancer, I thought constantly about riding. I daydreamed about the sensations of moving through the countryside on a bike, of the wind against my face. I yearned for the sense of well-being that riding gave me and the pleasant sensation of being spent after a long day. Riding up one of the Alps seemed like heaven compared to lying in a hospital bed drugged, parched and burned from the inside out. Before, I'd enjoyed riding and the living it provided me, but I hadn't truly appreciated it. After my near-death experience, when I confronted the possibility of never being able to ride again, my feelings for the sport multiplied.

When I was well enough, I'd take short rides around my neighbourhood in Austin. Or sometimes I'd go into my garage and turn on loud music, climb on an exercise bike and pedal furiously until I was covered with sweat. I rode to prove I wasn't dying.

Now I ride to prove that I'm alive. Each time I ride in the Tour, I prove that I survived cancer. I've survived it again, and again, and again, and again. Even in the midst of a hard day on the bike, beneath every pain and stress is the sense of relief and pleasure that I'm able to ride again. I ride to prove that in a scientific and highly mechanized era, the human body is still a marvel.

In cycling, there is no outer skin of metal to protect you from the elements. You have only your flimsy clothing, and this makes it a sport that is as sensuous as it is severe. The cyclist experiences great beauty – sublime views, the swooping exhilaration of a mountain descent – but there's a penalty on the body for cycling, too: a physical toll is taken in exchange for the beauty of the trip to remind you that you are human.

Cycling hurts in a dozen different ways. You're sore constantly. Sore neck, sore knees, sore hamstrings, sore calves. Cyclists get tendonitis all the time. You get it from crashing or from riding in a fixed position for hours on end. You wake up one morning and it's in an elbow or a knee. But absolutely the worst way to hurt on a bike is to get road rash, the result of your thin skin meeting asphalt and gravel. I've left pieces of myself over all the roads of Europe.

Road rash is what happens when you fall off a bike and skid on asphalt at 40 mph. We're not talking about a scraped knee. We're talking about rolling down crude rocky asphalt of northern France and skinning both sides of your entire body – front and back, too. It leaves you with scabby, nasty, scraped off skin – sometimes to the bone. It hurts. It hurts for days or weeks. It hurts so much you can't sleep. The mere touch of a sheet can make you, rolling over in bed, wake up and groan in the middle of the night, 'Ahhhhhh.' If you crash and get a bad case of road rash, it could mess you up for the rest of the Tour.

The worst case of road rash I ever had was in the 1995 Tour when I crashed during a stage to Dunkirk. It was high-speed pack finish, and some guy just came up out of nowhere and nailed me from the side. The bike was destroyed, and I went flying across the rough northern French pavement. I had to go to the hospital. I had raw scraped skin all over my body – up and down, left and right. I sat at the dinner table that night, and my friend Fabio Casartelli, the late Olympic champion, said, 'No way can you race.' I said, 'I'll be all right.' The next day I didn't see how I'd walk, let alone climb back on my bike. I managed to ride, but gingerly.

But there are also occasions when cycling feels effortless, inhumanly so. My friend George Hincapie, an American champion and my team-mate on the US Postal Service squad, has a saying when he is feeling really good: 'No chain.' The chain on the bike cranks the wheels and creates the tension in your legs that drives the bike forward. But imagine if you didn't have a chain. You'd spin nothing; air, which would feel really easy. So George and I have this thing:

'Man, can you check something for me?' he'll say.

'What?'

'I don't feel a chain,' he'd say. 'Is there a chain on my bike?'

It became shorthand, 'No chain.'

I'd say, 'Hey, how good do you feel today, George?'

'No chain, no chain.'

I'm awe-inspired by technology that outstrips human performance, and I credit science with saving my life. But a bicycle, no matter how elaborate the technology or how advanced the composite, remains driven by the body. There is something fundamental about a bike: a frame with a crank, a chain and two wheels, powered by nothing more than your own legs. On a bike, you are under your own power, directed by your own hand. Your wheel and motor is yourself.

All professional athletes have a relationship with the tools of their sport that transcends familiarity. There was a legend that baseballer

Ted Williams could see the seams on a fastball. It sounds perfectly legitimate to me. I know scores of stories about how athletes acquire hypersensitivities to the things they use. My friend Tiger Woods is phenomenal with golf clubs; what he's able to do bears no relation to the game of golf, as I know it. It's as though he's got more wires in his body when it comes to swinging a club. On occasion, Nike sends him drivers to test. He can hit a few balls on the range and give you a pretty good guess as to what the specs of the club are. Once, Nike gave him six drivers to choose from, and one was a little heavier than the rest by 2 grams, roughly the weight of a 1-dollar bill. He was able to pick it out without a gauge or scale.

Another time, Tiger was testing golf balls for the different levels of hardness in the dimpled covers. He simply bounced them off the face of his club and could tell by the feel where they ranked, hardest to softest, in perfect order. I've heard the same types of stories about tennis players. Hand Andre Agassi two rackets, and he'll hand one back to you. 'This one's heavier,' he'll say.

It's only natural, since I've been on a bike pretty much every day for the last two decades, that I have a sort of heightened sensory sensitivity to bikes. The mechanics on the US Postal Team call me 'Mister Millimetre' because I am so particular about the setup of my bike. Raise or lower the seat even a shade, and as soon I'm astride it, I'll say, 'Who screwed with my bike?'

Cyclists ask the bike to perform in ways most ordinary riders can't understand much less duplicate, so our equipment is naturally more highly specialized. The manufacturers make bikes and components for Tour riders that are also available to consumers, but it's questionable what percentage of riders should be riding such an elaborate racing rig.

Tour cyclists have higher than average tactile skills; they know how to use a bike in ways other people can't fathom because they're aboard one for so many hours in so many conditions. My bikes are made for the arduous circumstances of the Tour de France, a race so long it's said you have to get a haircut halfway through. I use the same basic model and design that you see in a shop, but it's set for high performance racing and also for my own particular physique and riding abilities. Some parts of my equipment are pretty normal and others are unique and wouldn't benefit any rider but me. There are a thousand small variances from one person's bike to the next, and mine only suit me. People want to talk about the specs of my bikes, but that's really only part of the story. Bikes are like DNA – there are a 100 or more things that have to be matched up in certain ways in order to yield a certain performance, and they're synergistic.

It's hard to say how I arrived at the setup of my bike: I'm very methodical. I tinker, I experiment, and I learn as much as possible: I want to understand a great-looking piece of design and how best to use it. I spend hours in wind tunnels playing with my positioning and testing new components, searching for an extra second here or there on a time-trial bike or a climbing bike. Sometimes it's highly technical stuff, involving power-to-weight ratios, moments of inertia, centres of gravity, the spokes of a wheel, or the shape of a piece of tubing. It goes on and on.

But it's like a sunset – I can't describe how all of the things go together, but I know it when I see it, and, most importantly, I know it when I feel it. To me, the body will always trump technology.

The British author and cycling enthusiast Graeme Fife wrote of cycling, 'Where high performance machines are in competition, their drivers will always have to concede some of their triumph to the machine, or ought to; there are some disagreeable exceptions. But the bicycle can never make so much of a difference that we will call "Foul" because one rider has a demonstrably, an intrinsically superior machine to another. On the road, at any rate.' In other words, a motor-racing driver can win a race because he has a better engine or parts or a superior car in general, even if he's not the best driver. But on a bike, all men are equal, with no clear mechanical advantage. It therefore becomes a pure test of endurance and will. The body itself is the more important machine, and whoever has trained it and attuned it most thoroughly – not just his arms and legs but also his mind and heart – will be the victor. That's why a race like the Tour de France is traditionally regarded as not just a contest of speed or endurance, but also a journey or crusade.

We live in a generation of brilliant technologists; we've got a lot of new tools and materials other generations didn't have. But we aren't the first brilliant generation. In 150-odd years of bicycle design and use, the bike has evolved and certain things have been proven to work. They are as true today as they were 50 years ago. A bicycle is a classic design, and the basic principles on which it works – of power-to-weight ratios and centrifugal force – haven't changed, no matter how computer-modelled and milled the parts are.

The basic concept of a body borne through space freely, with the aid of nothing but a crank, two wheels and arms and legs, remains poetically unchanged.

What better way to see the world?

CHAPTER 1

WHAT EVERY KID WANTS

by Bill Strickland

COMING OF AGE

Every child's dream:
a dog, a bike and an
endless summer day.

One sparkling bright summer day when I was 11, my bike and I ran away from home. I forgot long ago what childish sin I committed but I know that as punishment my bike and I, unbearably, were to be separated for some time.

I'd been given the off-brand BMX bike as a present only that Spring. It had an oval number plate, 'official' race stickers and crash pads on the crossbar and top tube. The pro-style nubs on the right grip had worn off; my friends and I all rigged our right grips to twist in our hands like motorcycle throttles without sliding off the handlebar. I ran a playing card against the spokes, of course, choosing replacements according to my mood on whatever day the old paper rectangle finally shredded away. (I favoured aces and jacks.)

Even with *parents just behind, freedom is always close at hand on a bicycle.*

Samuel Beckett *recalled an early bicycle with great fondness.*

Years later, as a racing cyclist – a 'serious' cyclist – I would learn to despise kickstands for their extra weight and 'uncool' aura. But on my BMXer, I showcased the kickstand by spray-painting it metallic silver like an exhaust pipe. The back edge of the seat was curled and crisped; a friend of mine had convinced me that by taping model-rocket engines to the underside of our saddles we could get a burst of speed upon ignition. (All we got were scorched seats and flat tyres – and the admiration of every kid in the neighbourhood.)

It's not unusual that I can remember every detail of my bike. Samuel Beckett, describing a bike of his youth, wrote 'To describe it at length would be a pleasure. It had a little red horn instead of the bell. To blow this horn was for me a real pleasure, almost a vice.'

As a get-away vehicle, *the bicycle is unsurpassed.*

Yet even more vivid than my memory of that bike is how it called to me that day. I'd been riding for about four years but felt myself newly mobile on that big-kid's bicycle – it was never meant to accept training wheels, and it had never known me when I couldn't ride. That was a time when we rode our bikes in packs, kin to the dogs that were also free to roam neighbourhoods at will. You rode your bike, dropped it wherever a game started, rode it another block, dropped it, and played more. Your bike was always there. Occasionally a group of kids would go out expressly to 'ride' but most often our bikes were not merely a childish game but our accomplices in the entire adventure of being children.

So, picture a day from your childhood, a perfect day – bright, shiny, filled with friends and bikes. Your legs kick. You squint into a headwind of your own creation and gulp at it in greedy joy, like a dog with its head stuck out of a car window. That was my day. The bike rolled with a kind of righteous inevitability; we might go anywhere. My own road disappeared under the rear wheel, then the familiar streets of my neighbourhood, then the routes my parents drove. I saw a lake. There were no lakes near our home.

My bike and I stopped. I kickstanded it, left it leaning against itself, wheel turned as if it were watching me, curious.

While I played at the water's edge, someone stole my bike.

The perfect portrait
of childhood: bikes,
sun and smiles all
round.

INHERENT OR LEARNED

There is no more useful toy than a bicycle; no vehicle more playful, no piece of exercise equipment so liberating, and no symbol of childhood that so powerfully and paradoxically signals the coming of adulthood.

Your bike takes you down the driveway, over the kerb, away from the steady hand of your father, then beyond arm's reach and, eventually, further. As far as you want to go. The significance is not just the distance that grows between the hand and the bike, but the speed. Even wobbly, unsure, turning to look over your shoulder to see if you truly are riding on your own – even then you are, for the first time in your life, faster than Mum and Dad.

The first *pedal strokes are a timeless rite of passage.*

GREG LEMOND
The Original American Legend

Since its inception in 1903, the Tour de France had been dominated by Europeans. It took the considerable abilities of American Greg LeMond to prove that there were cyclists from other nations who could contend for the title. His memorable victory in 1996 brought the Tour de France to mainstream America.

Born in 1961, LeMond began racing at the age of 14 and turned pro by 19. He swiftly established himself among the European elite, becoming the first non-European to win the Tour de France in 1986 at the tender age of 25. The next year, LeMond's brother-in-law accidentally shot him while they were out hunting. Sixty lead pellets penetrated his body, collapsing his right lung and striking his liver, intestine, diaphragm, kidney and heart. The following two years were a bleak struggle marred by poor performances and subsequent health problems as he tried to race once again.

Not ready to quit, he entered the Tour de France in 1989. Although 30 shotgun pellets remained in his body, LeMond was back on top. After more than 2,000 miles (3,220 km), including the towering Pyrenees and Alps, he sat just 50 seconds behind first place. Equipped with aerobars and an aerodynamic helmet (both unheard of in the Tour at that time), LeMond did the impossible: he beat the leader by 8 seconds – averaging an unparalleled 34 miles per hour – in the race's final time trial. The next year, he won once more, crowning one of sport's most renowned comebacks. Today, LeMond remains an innovator, lending his expertise to a line of road and exercise bikes and cycling accessories.

VITAL STATS

NATIONALITY: American

DATE OF BIRTH: 26 June 1961

CAREER VICTORY HIGHLIGHTS: Tour de France: 1986, 1989, 1990; World Champion: 1983, 1989; Dauphiné Libéré: 1983; Coors Classic: 1981, 1985; Tour du Pont: 1992

Keep your will *from wobbling,*
and your bike will always run true.

The bike, the first vehicle we master, teaches us the costs and consequences of propulsion. Fall and you scrape not just your knee but your shiny new machine as well. Forget to inflate your tyre and you get a flat. Leave the bike behind the car and it gets mangled.

Some people go so far as to equate the lessons of balance that we must master with, well, lessons of balance. 'I finally determined that all failures were from a wobbling will rather than a wobbling wheel,' wrote Frances Willard, a turn-of-the-century American women's rights activist who learned to ride a bicycle at 50. It could be that when we learn just how much speed will take us around a corner safely, we're learning something about how to manage a career 30 years hence. If so, it is not at all apparent in the moment and barely there with hindsight, which makes it the best sort of cosmic lesson.

A bike is the one Christmas present every child receives, the birthday gift your parents shouldn't have been able to afford, the unfulfilled dream in the shop window that comes true one time for all of us. A child on a bike is a wish fulfilled and a promise still in the making.

A little girl *who perhaps has yet to discover the pleasures of riding a bike.*

'As a kid, I had a dream – I wanted to own my own bicycle,' said John Lennon, in an early interview with *Bicycling* magazine. 'When I got the bicycle, I must have been the happiest boy in Liverpool, maybe in the world. I lived for that bike. Most kids left their bikes in the backyard at night. Not me. I insisted on taking mine indoors and the first night I even kept it in my bed.'

When our parents give us our first bike it is also a metaphor of what they must do to raise us: provide us with the tools we need to leave them. And though the process of learning to ride seems to be almost guaranteed – more of us can ride than swim – it's impossible to overstate the difficulty of what we actually accomplish when we pedal off on our own.

As a child *John Lennon dreamed of having a bike; although probably not one that was white and covered with flowers.*

Lesson 1: *learn to go.*
Lesson 2: learn to stop.

'The machine appears uncomplicated but the theories governing its motion are nightmarish,' bicycle physicist Chester Kyle explained to *Bicycling* magazine. 'Some things can't be easily defined by physics and mathematics. The interactions of the body, mind, muscles, terrain, gravity, air and bicycle are so complex that they defy exact mathematical solutions. The feel and handling of a bike borders on art. Like the violin, it's been largely designed by touch, inspiration and experimentation.' *(continued on page 32)*

A bicycle *appears uncomplicated, but it's a veritable physics lesson in motion.*

Light Years Ahead of His Time

Born in 1879, Albert Einstein is arguably one of the greatest geniuses who ever lived. His keen observation of the world around him laid the foundation for an explosion of scientific theory. By simply casting his eyes skyward, Einstein dreamed up notions of time and space that forever changed the way we view the universe. And his most acclaimed discovery – the Theory of Relativity – came to him while out on a simple bike ride.

While pedalling at night, Einstein observed that the bobbing beam cast from his headlamp always travelled at the same speed, whether he was cruising at a fast pace or coasting to a stop. The theory – that light from a moving source has the same velocity as light from a stationary source – was born on that ride. 'I thought of it while riding my bicycle,' remains a familiar quote of Einstein's to this day. Another favourite saying – 'Life is like riding a bicycle. To keep your balance, you must keep moving' – was indicative of the joyful, compassionate scientist's love of the bicycle. Early in his schooling at Munich University, he would take bicycle tours with fellow scientists to contemplate the world at large. And during his final years, while at Princeton, in the USA, during the early 1950s, when the automobile was the customary mode of transportation, Einstein chose his trusty steed over any other modern engineering marvels. Indeed, the most enduring image of the wild-haired genius is that of him cruising around on his bicycle with his infectious grin, gleefully imagining the next revolutionary idea.

Einstein *thought the bicycle was relatively fantastic.*

Not only was *riding a bicycle a means of illustrating*
Einstein's theories, it was also one of his favourite activities.

A bicycle is a remarkable feat of engineering – it can carry 10 times its own weight and uses energy more efficiently than a soaring eagle. Yet a seven-year-old can master its mechanics. Indeed, it's the first machine many of us ever take apart and successfully (or not) reassemble. There's something about its lines, some feeling inherent in its circles and curves that appeals to us. Our longing for a shiny new bicycle lives somewhere beyond the practical. Toys hit children in waves of popularity and resurgence: count on the yo-yo to become trendy again every decade or so and hold on to your scooters for the next revival. The bicycle never goes out of fashion. A first bicycle lives in us like a first kiss. A best friend. Our favourite dog.

Riding allows us *to see more of the world around us and, most importantly, to contemplate.*

Mike Burrows, a designer who's created some of the most stunning modern bicycles, admits perplexity and awe, as well: 'Some things need to be drawn before they can be designed and understood. Others need to be made first, and the bicycle is the latter,' he says. 'It is inconceivable that the principles involved in riding a bicycle could ever be theorized first. It's far more likely that the principles of balance related to the bicycle were discovered by someone playing around with things that had wheels. Put simply, a cyclist proceeds in a series of falls that are compensated for by steering the bicycle back under the centre of gravity. This complex principle cannot be analysed by computers but is done automatically by us, clever apes. And it is a skill that once learned is never forgotten.' *(continued on page 36)*

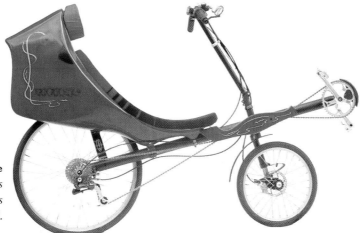

The principles of balance
work equally well for cycles of various design, such as this recumbent model.

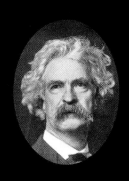

'Learn to ride
a bicycle.
You will not regret it
if you live.'

MARK TWAIN

LIFE LESSONS

We pine for our lost bicycles. Those that are stolen teach us a lesson about the adult world we're riding so carelessly into. A bike taken is a bike forever elevated in memory. The story is different for the bikes we abandon, which is what happens most often. We leave our bikes as inevitably as we leave our childhood.

I've often wondered if children can sense all that's in a bike, if that sort of ancestral knowledge might explain our intense attraction to these strange vehicles. Is this a modern version of an ordained pairing like caveman and canine? Perhaps the power lies not in the bicycle itself but in the adults who pass on the artifact; maybe we imbue the bicycle with something of what we know. In this way, riding a bicycle is most like crossing a bridge from childhood to adulthood. A child can pedal across the bridge as often and as far as he or she wants and always return back to being a child – not so once you drive across that bridge with a car.

Falling *may be the first lesson of riding.*

So strong *is the connection that we may pine for our lost or damaged bicycles for the rest of our lives.*

The young at heart
can rekindle their
love of bicycling.

As adults, of course, we can cross that bridge, too. Back. Because, if we're very lucky and rediscover cycling when we're older, the bike gets a chance to perform its miracle of liberation again. Just as the bike lets the child glimpse adulthood, so an adult on a bike can sightsee youth. The appeal is not, as it originally was, the magnificence of the distance we can achieve, but the intimacy of the trip. As adults, we might never ride our bikes further than we drive to work (and certainly few of us ride our bikes further than we could drive in a single day) but a simple five-mile spin through the local area can take us much further than we actually travelled. It's not so much the unknown world that beckons as the freshness of the familiar world you've come to inhabit. You become acquainted with cracks in the road, with kerbs, with dogs that confront you. You run your wheels across skittering leaves, drop your head and milk the speed of a fine downhill. Ride a bike around the area where you grew up and you can almost hear your mother calling you in for dinner.

Ride for an hour and you burn enough to enjoy the extra slices of cheese with the wine. Ride for a whole Saturday afternoon and you no longer have to think twice about that night's chocolate dessert – you can indulge as guiltlessly and guilelessly as a child. Ride most of the Sundays for a year and you regain the metabolism of a child, the unthinking ability to incinerate whatever's put in front of you.

(continued on page 45)

Take the kids *for a spin and reward yourself with a triple-fudge sundae.*

The bicycle *sets us on a path to adventure and discovery.*

'Toleration is the greatest gift of the mind; it requires the same effort of the brain that it takes to balance oneself on a bicycle.'

HELEN KELLER

The sidecar *attached to this early bicycle provides a great vantage point from which to view the world.*

A bicycle moves at the ideal pace to see the world: fast enough to outrace boredom, slowly enough to absorb detail. On a bike, you become part of your environment rather than hurtling through it in a car or plane. You can dawdle or blur your eyes with speed and either way be confident that you're moving at a human pace.

Whether departing on *a grand adventure or returning from a short trip, riding gets us where we need to go.*

The bicycle is an equalizer; it opens its magic to any of us. Its frame supports people too heavy to walk or jog; its smooth circular motion soothes damaged knees and welcomes those who can't participate in impact- or contact-based sports; blind people hop onto the backs of tandems for the sheer thrill of the ride.

Be it in the heart *of the city or on a deserted beach, put two people on bikes and there's bound to be some horseplay.*

Hemingway *loved bikes and the unique perspective they provide.*

Like all aerobic sports, cycling releases endorphins. But there's some evidence that the rhythm of pedalling itself helps the brain mimic the calming and restorative state of deep meditation.

Ernest Hemingway and Pablo Picasso loved bikes throughout their lives (and put cycling into their art). Albert Einstein said he thought of the Theory of Relativity while riding his bike. Simone de Beauvoir recounted that Jean-Paul Sartre 'much preferred riding a bicycle to walking. He would amuse himself by sprinting on hills. On level stretches, he pedalled with such indifference that on two or three occasions he landed in ditches'.

We never forget how to ride a bike, so the saying goes, and it's so true that it seems an oddity of humanity: why does this particular machine hold such a spot in our souls? Just try to climb trees or turn cartwheels like you did when you were 7. But abandon your bike, banish the idea of cycling from your life for 20 years, 30 years, then pick up a bike, throw a leg over it, hop on and pedal off. It just feels right.

'To ride a bicycle properly is very like a love affair,' wrote H. G. Wells in his cycling novel, *The Wheels of Chance*. 'Chiefly, it is a matter of faith. Believe you can do it, and the thing is done; doubt, and for the life of you, you cannot.'

(continued on page 52)

H. G. Wells *believed riding a bike was 'very like a love affair'.*

Party in the Heartland

It started out innocently enough. In 1973, John Karras, the feature writer for the *Des Moines Register* challenged Don Kaul, author of the *Register*'s 'Over the Coffee' column to ride his bicycle across the the State of Iowa, USA, and write about the experience. Kaul agreed, with the stipulation that Karras come along. They invited readers to join them, and on 26 August 300 riders set off. Six days later, 114 steadfast cyclists pulled into the final town. In the weeks that followed, the *Register* was flooded with calls from cyclists who missed the event, pleading for an encore. They got it. The second year, 1,700 showed up, and a tradition was born. On the surface, RAGBRAI (Register's Annual Great Bicycle Ride Across Iowa) is like any bicycle tour. Riders start at point A, in this case a town along the Missouri River, and end at point B, which in RAGBRAI is a town along the Mississippi River. What sets it apart is the carnival-like atmosphere. A typical day of RAGBRAI will consist of 60 to 70 miles (96 to 113 km), with a town stop every 10 to 15 miles (12 to 24 km).

John Karras

Hosting towns open their bars, set up booths and attractions, and welcome riders to shop, eat and party. Along the route there are DJs, music, beer tents and raucous festivities.

Riders dress up (or down) in traffic-stopping costumes and often ride together as 'teams'. Some ride the entire stretch; others jump in for a day or two mid-State.

Following the *Register*'s lead, more than 40 other States across the US have hosted their own tours, although none has risen to the notoriety of the original. Some 30 years later, RAGBRAI is still rolling strong, with devoted fans signing up a year in advance to ensure their spot in one of America's greatest parties on wheels.

More than *30 years ago, it started as a dare; today it's the most well-known multi-day bike tour in America.*

Then, of course, when it's time for us to pass along the love of cycling, we see the lesson from the other side of the bridge. To run alongside a wobbly but speedy child on a bike is to confront the conundrum of parenting: how much support and how much freedom? In which balance lies success?

Teaching a child *to ride is to confront the central conundrum of parenting: how much support versus how much freedom?*

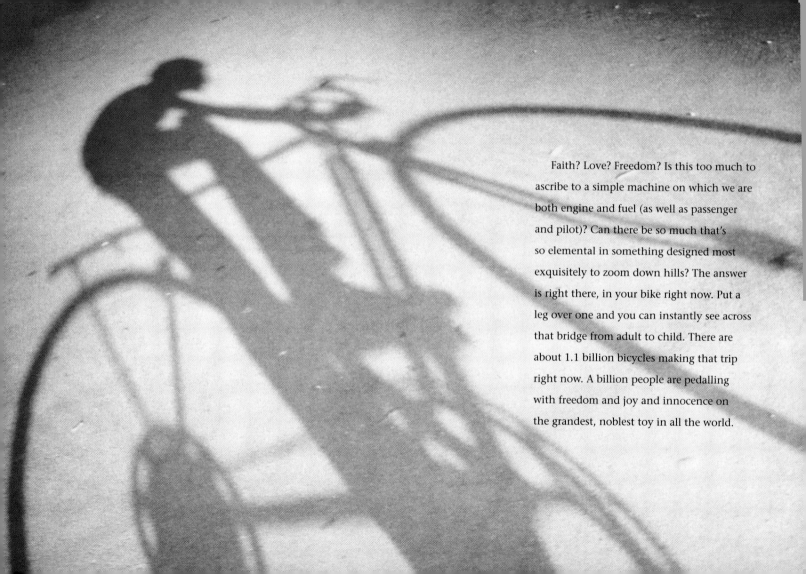

Faith? Love? Freedom? Is this too much to ascribe to a simple machine on which we are both engine and fuel (as well as passenger and pilot)? Can there be so much that's so elemental in something designed most exquisitely to zoom down hills? The answer is right there, in your bike right now. Put a leg over one and you can instantly see across that bridge from adult to child. There are about 1.1 billion bicycles making that trip right now. A billion people are pedalling with freedom and joy and innocence on the grandest, noblest toy in all the world.

CHAPTER 2

BICYCLING CULTURE

By Mark Riedy and Joe Lindsey

WHY WE RIDE

Bicycles are the most efficient form of transportation known; affordable by almost 90 per cent of the world's population, they can go almost anywhere, often more quickly, than any other conveyance. But none of that gets to the root of why we spend large amounts of money on equipment, why we stare at photographs of beautiful spots to ride, or why we transport our bikes thousands of miles simply to ride them in a different place.

Simply put, we ride because we love the ride. The act of riding is at once an elegantly simple and tremendously complex sensation: it is the culmination of hundreds of thoughts and emotions – escape, love of nature, exercise – and, at times, the complete *absence* of thought and emotion, a singular focus that allows for no distraction and spares no mental or physical faculty. The myriad kinds of bikes, riders and riding, speak to the multi-layered experience that is cycling. It is different things to us all.

A bike ride is *the culmination of hundreds of thoughts and emotions and at times the complete absence of thought and emotion.*

RACING

So enmeshed are bikes and bicycle racing that one cannot track the history of the one without tracking the history of the other. Yet for many cyclists, the only contact they have with a bicycle race might be a clip of the Tour de France on television or a shot of the current champion on the cover of a newspaper or magazine.

The first bike race was held in Paris not long after the Michaux brothers became the first to attach pedals to a 'bicycle', and today bicycles are raced in every place imaginable – from the urban retreats of parks in cities like London and Melbourne to the untamed plains of West Africa. In increasingly complicated times, the simple sport of bicycle racing continues to strike a romantic chord in hearts the world over.

Bicycle racing
and its timeless brand of escapism has struck a romantic chord with the public since the Victorian era in which it began.

TRACK RACING

Due to the lack of good roads and the rudimentary technology used on early bicycles, track racing was the first widely practised form of competition. As the world entered the 20th century, track racing had become the most popular spectator sport and fittingly it featured the highest-paid athletes. In 1920s America auditoriums such as Madison Square Garden in New York City and the Chicago Stadium drew enormous, celebrity filled crowds.

At the turn of the 20th century, *when track racing was at the height of its popularity, track racers could earn huge salaries.*

MAJOR TAYLOR
Breaking Cultural Barriers

In a sport that is still largely dominated by white men, Marshall W. Taylor was to cycling what Jessie Owens was to athletics, overcoming segregation, racism and bigotry to compete in the sport at which he excelled.

Born to a poor rural family near Indianapolis, Indiana, USA, Taylor first came into the sport as an entertainer. Hired by a bike shop at the age of 13 to perform bicycle stunts in a soldier's uniform, he earned his lifelong nickname, 'Major'. Four years later, he got his big break, when his boss, well-known bike racer Louis 'Birdie' Munger, decided to put Major on the professional circuit.

Despite his speed and determination, Major was plagued early on by racism. Various tracks and championships banned his participation. Then in 1899, at just 19 years of age, he broke through racial barriers by competing in and winning the world 1-mile championship. He went on to dominate the American and European cycling scene, defeating the best cyclists in the world. He also enjoyed a successful season touring Australia. During the peak of his career, Taylor was earning a dizzying $3,000 a day racing – ranking him among the highest-paid athletes of his time.

Sadly, life after track racing proved less kind. Failed business ventures and ailing health sapped his fortune. In 1932, aged 53, he died in a charity ward and was buried in an unmarked grave. Wanting a better end for a forgotten hero, Frank Schwinn, founder of the Schwinn Bicycle Company, and other professional racers pitched in to move Taylor's remains to a more prominent grave in Illinois. Today, the Major Taylor Velodrome in Indianapolis, USA, is a monument to his achievements.

VITAL STATS

NATIONALITY: American

DATE OF BIRTH: 26 November 1878

CAREER VICTORY HIGHLIGHTS: 1-Mile Championship: 1899
US Sprint Championship: 1898, 1899, 1900

New York's *Madison Square Garden was originally built to hold Six-Day races.*

The world of track racing and velodromes reached its zenith between 1900 and 1940 when Six-Day racing, where two-rider teams raced multiple events over a number of days, was hugely popular. Across America there were major Six-Day events and lavish stadiums, such as Madison Square Garden in New York, were built to house them. In Europe, smoky stadiums in Amsterdam, Moscow, Berlin, Copenhagen and a dozen or more smaller cities still host successful Six-Day events that are, as ever, heavily wagered upon.

A Multi-Day Test of Mettle

At the turn of the 19th century, in the glory days of track racing, audiences loved velodrome events so much they couldn't get enough – literally. At Madison Square Garden stadium in New York City, track events known as Six-Day races were created to keep the action going, and going. Two-man teams would circle the track for a gruelling six days and nights. Before long, these endless suffer-fests were the rage throughout America and Europe.

Then like all crazes, the Six-Day phenomenon started to cool. Although the rules dictated that only one team member needed to be on the track at any given time, allowing the other to take a fuel or nap break, racers and fans alike grew weary after 144 successive hours. The race format was refined to keep the spirit but also to maintain the excitement. Today's Six-Day races take place over six consecutive evenings. Instead of one long race stretching through the night, various mini-races are staged: *points races,* where sprinters race for the finish line at the ring of a bell; *miss-and-out elimination races,* where the last rider across the line is pulled from the field and *motor-paced events.* At the heart of Six-Day evening events is the

Madison, named after Madison Square Garden where the event was first held. This long, multi-lap race features team members on the track circling at top speed, while their team-mates hover slowly along the boards, waiting until their partner needs a break, at which time they dive down to the field and clasp hands with their team-mate, who literally flings them into the ongoing race.

Today, Six-Day track events remain a staple of the cycling season. In Europe, they are often accompanied by week-long festivities featuring fairs, bands and plenty of beer. In Australia, Six-Day races have been replaced by more generalized track carnivals involving a mixture of events.

The original Six-Day format, *where teams of two riders went for 144 hours without stopping, didn't allow for much time to rest.*

Track racers differ from other types of cyclists in their raw athleticism. Because there are no hills to climb, track racers focus on building as much muscle mass and power as possible.

Known as the 'Race of Truth', the Hour Record is the most prestigious title in all of cycling. To claim it, a cyclist must do one deceptively simple thing: ride a bicycle around a velodrome for one hour, faster than anyone who has ever walked the face of the earth.

So elusive is it that only two dozen men have ever held the title in the past 110 years. Among them the giants of the sport: Tour de France founder Henri Desgrange; the greatest Italian cyclist of all time, Fausto Coppi; and five-time Tour de France winner, Eddy Merckx of Belgium.

In the early days, as now, *Velodromes were for amateurs and professionals alike.*

After smashing the record in 1993, British time-trial specialist Chris Boardman swapped ideas for refined aerodynamic positions and equipment with Scotsman Graeme Obree as both set new high marks. The International Cycling Union (Union Cycliste Internationale, or UCI), cycling's governing body, banned the advances and in effect turned the clock back to 1972, reinstating Merckx's 49.432 kilometre record and requiring technologically identical equipment to that used by Merckx for any future attempts. Astride a simple steel bike with no aero wheels or handlebars, Boardman still managed to extend Merckx's record by just 10 metres in September 2000. His record of 49.441 kilometres in an hour still stands.

(continued on page 72)

British racer Chris Boardman *has broken the Hour Record three times.*

VELODROMES
What Goes Around Comes Around

Soon after men invented the bicycle, they had to decide who was the fastest on one – and the velodrome was born. Generally constructed of wood or cement, although sometimes grass and earth, velodromes are oval tracks used for bicycle racing. They're usually around 333.3 metres (1,090 ft) in length and consist of two straights linked with two turns. The turns are steeply banked so riders can dive down off the top of the track at great speeds.

Because of the fast pace, photo-finish wins and propensity for spectacular crashes, velodrome, or track, racing became wildly popular in Europe and Japan as well as the US and Australia at the end of the 19th century. By the 1920s, nearly every city in America and Europe had a velodrome and indoor racing was one of the most popular,

celebrity-packed spectator sports. But as with all bright stars, track racing eventually lost its lustre. The development of the car had a strong impact and by the 1940s most indoor tracks were being torn down.

Today, particularly in Europe and Japan, thousands of fans flock to velodromes to watch (and often bet on) track-racing events of all kinds. In the US, velodrome popularity is on the upswing once more, with about 20 tracks nationwide and more in the works.

Ensuring the enduring popularity of the velododrome in their country, the Japanese have contributed the Keirin race, a motor-paced event until the last lap when the motorbike pulls off the track and the riders sprint madly to the line. In Japan, huge amounts of money are bet on races, while professional Keirin riders command

impressive salaries. Keirin races have become staple features of European, American and Australian track events.

With no brakes *and four corners per lap, track racing is a thrill-a-second sport.*

For his 1993 record, *Chris Boardman's French-made Corima was at the cutting edge of technology.*

CHRIS BOARDMAN
Master Against the Clock

For many racers, the hardest test they face is the time trial. There are no team-mates to draft, competitors to chase or adversaries breathing down your back. It's just you, the clock and whatever will and power you can muster for the allotted time or distance. Because it exposes riders for their talents alone, cyclists deem it the 'Race of Truth'. And Chris Boardman might be the most honest cyclist who ever lived.

Boardman began riding as a teenager and quickly qualified to join one of the most prestigious clubs in Britain, the Manchester Wheelers. As a young racer, he stacked up 30 national titles and became the man to beat on the UK time-trial scene, with only one competitor, Scotland's Graeme Obree, ever nudging him out of the top spot. In 1992, he stamped his mark internationally with a gold medal victory in the 4,000-metre individual pursuit at the Barcelona Olympics.

Throughout the 1990s, Boardman proved he was the fastest man on wheels. He won three Tour de France prologues, clocking the fastest time ever recorded in the 1994 Tour. He captured his first world Hour Record in 1993; then after a bad crash in 1995, he came back to reclaim the title in a crushing 2000 performance that still stands unbeaten today.

Boardman might still be beating time on his bike were it not for being diagnosed with a brittle-bone disease that forced his retirement. Most agree, however, that although the rider has been forced from his bike, his records will probably remain for many years to come.

VITAL STATS

NATIONALITY: British

DATE OF BIRTH: 26 August 1968

CAREER VICTORY HIGHLIGHTS: World Hour Record: 1993, 2000; World 4,000-metre pursuit: 1996; Tour de France prologue: 1994 (race record, fastest prologue), 1997 and 1998; Olympic 4,000-metre pursuit: 1992

ROAD RACING

Romantic, tradition-bound and unmistakably European, bicycle road racing is one of the most dramatic and intricate sports practised today. The physical demands that it places on the riders as well as the staggering natural beauty of the 'stadiums' in which it is played out have made road racing one of the most watched sports in the world. Whether it's the highest paved road in the Alps, the thin ribbon of asphalt along the Italian Riviera, a 500-year-old cobblestone path in Belgium's low country or the diamond-studded Parisian glory of the Champs Elysées, cycling's drama is acted out on a stage as varied and dramatic as the sport itself.

Lance Armstrong's *US Postal Service Team leads the field in the 2002 Tour de France.*

'Centuries', or 100-mile rides, are legion to road riders. There are hundreds of organized century rides and they've been around as long as the sport itself; no one even has records of who was the first to ride 100 miles at a single clip. But it's a baseline for serious cyclists, a commencement ceremony marking the transition from a person who rides bikes to a cyclist. A century makes sense to people who don't ride; lesser distances don't sound as impressive and larger ones are a pure abstraction. A century is a universal yardstick for all cyclists and non-cyclists alike. Personal physical accomplishments such as riding a century or riding across an entire country, are often compounded by other kinds of satisfaction, such as raising money for a cause.

One of the earliest recorded bicycle races was a group of riders competing for a prize in Munich in 1829, shortly after Baron von Drais had introduced his machine. In 1869, a Parisian cycling club (*Le Veloce-Club de Paris*) and early French cycling magazine *Velocipede Illustré* organized a race between Paris and Rouen in which nearly 300 competitors took part. It was from beginnings such as these that the Grand Tours of France, Italy and Spain would develop, and racers such as Italy's Fausto Coppi, France's Jacques Anquetil, Belgium's Eddy Merckx and Spain's Miguel Indurain became household names.

Developing later with the bike boom of the 1970s and ending with the emergence of mountain biking and triathlons in the mid-1980s, road racing in America experienced incredible popularity among athletes looking for something different from the traditional American sports. Yet, from the time of American Greg LeMond's third and final Tour de France victory in 1990 and Lance Armstrong's first in 1999, interest in the sport declined in the United States, with the spotlight and sponsorship money falling to the more trendy off-road events. Lance Armstrong's staggering personal victory

Road racing *epitomizes the drama of the open road, with crowds of spectators and hair-raising turns.*

over cancer and his five consecutive Tour de France victories between 1999 and 2003 have renewed enthusiasm for road racing and riding across America.

With fan clubs, corporate endorsement deals and political influence, today's professional road racers are the rock stars of the cycling world. Sponsors such as Deutsche Telekom, Panasonic, Renault, Peugeot and Motorola have brought big money into the sport. Currently, Lance Armstrong, the highest-paid cyclist ever, earns more than $10 million (£6.2 million) per year in endorsements from corporate giants such as Coke, Nike, Subaru and cancer-drug manufacturer Bristol-Myers Squibb.

Unfortunately, professional cycling will have to overcome the stigma of a sport marred by the use of illegal, performance-enhancing drugs if it is to maintain its global following. In the past five years, a number of champions and several major races, including the 1998 Tour de France, have been marked by illegal doping scandals – dramas that for many fans make the sport every bit as much of a farce as professional wrestling.

Lance Armstrong *is always very much in demand for autographs.*

CYCLO-CROSS

Traditionally a way for road racers to train in the cold and wet of the winter off-season, cyclo-cross is part road racing, part mountain biking and part cross-country running. With its European roots, esoteric equipment and singular physical challenge, cyclo-cross is popular in Europe and has a committed cult following in North America. At the turn of the century, Daniel Gousseau, a private in the French Army who would ride his safety bicycle on trails normally used by horse riders as a way to stay fit in the winter, began the practice that would evolve into the sport of cyclo-cross. By 1924, there was an international cyclo-cross racing scene spearheaded by Gousseau and the French Cycling Union, of which he became Secretary General. In the 1950s, the sport exploded, crowning its first world champion and

Esoteric equipment
*and a singular
physical challenge
make cyclo-cross
a cult classic.*

extending the international circuit throughout Europe.

Cyclo-cross is a type of cycling that, thanks to its devoted followers, draws a lot of attention within the cycling community at large. The most traditionally minded group of racers, cyclo-crossers are known for their vintage wool jerseys and love of strong, dark beer.

Cyclo-cross is one of the most accessible forms of cycle sport. Races are as much social outings as sporting events, with a relaxed, informal atmosphere. Entries are usually accepted on the day. The World Championships are held in late January or early February each year. Crowds of 20- to 30,000 are not uncommon, especially when held in the cyclo-cross heartlands of Belgium and Holland.

The single-speed mountain-bike racing scene that has blossomed around the world is arguably a direct descendant of the cyclo-cross community's desire for simple technology and difficult riding conditions. Spearheaded by UK-based magazine *The Outcast*, single-speed racing follows the cyclo-cross format for off-road riding, but only bikes with a single gear, as opposed to the 27 gears of a standard mountain bike, are allowed.

Cyclo-cross *competitors race though the mud with their bikes.*

Freewheeling, *fun and dirty, mountain-bike racing combines a love of sport with a love of the outdoors.*

MOUNTAIN AND OFF-ROAD RACING

The controversy surrounding the mountain bike's true inventor – was it Gary Fisher, Joe Breeze, a group of Parisians in the 1950s, or even turn-of-the-century off-roaders? – points to the fact that modern mountain biking wasn't so much a technical evolution as a complete social revolution. 'We were doing something no one else would. Most Marin County, California, residents didn't go up on Mount Tamalpais, so we had it to ourselves. We did and brought along on the rides things that you wouldn't on a road ride – dogs, a full lunch, frisbees, smokes, etc.,' said fat-tyre pioneer Gary Fisher, of the early days of modern mountain biking. Unable to assimilate their new culture into cycling's traditional social structure, mountain bikers of the mid- to late 1980s created their own vocabulary and dress, and established races that are now legendary such as the Repack Downhill, the UCI World Championships and the 24 Hours of Moab.

Mountain-bike pioneer *Gary Fisher rests on the trails of Mount Tamalpais.*

A massive string *of racers shreds an alpine descent.*

Mountain-bike racing *was first featured as an Olympic discipline at the 1996 games in Atlanta, USA. Here riders start the 2000 Olympic race in Sydney, Australia.*

For the most part, it was mountain-bike racing that pushed the fat-tyre scene into the spotlight. Led by early champions such as Joe Murray, Ned Overend, Jacquie Phelan and Juli Furtado, mountain-bike racing tapped into the public's thirst for adventure and pushed the culture to unimagined heights. The apotheosis of this was in 1996 when cross-country mountain-bike racing was featured at the Olympic Games for the first time ever. Held in Atlanta, USA, the '96 Olympics, put the mountain bike on display in front of the world, but ever since, cross-country racing and the group of athletes that practise it have taken a back seat to more adrenalin-fuelled, television-friendly forms of competition such as downhill racing, mountain cross, trials and slalom. In fact, as mountain biking gained mainstream popularity, many at the sport's core looked for new and original forms of expression. Soon, fringe events like single speed and adventure racing were attracting more and more people.

Canadian Alison Sydor *leads at the '96 Olympics in Atlanta, closely followed by American Juli Furtado.*

FREERIDING

It's hard to say whether the dramatic improvements in mountain-bike technology over the past decade made the freeride movement possible or whether freeriders pushed the technology to accommodate their fast, loose and out-of-control riding style. The loosely bound, danger-loving freeride scene developed in Canada on Vancouver's 'North Shore' in the early 1990s and spread throughout the world thanks to the popularity of videos like the *Kranked* series.

Over dirt, ditch, water or wood *freeriding makes the most of the challenges of the forest.*

RIVA DEL GARDA FESTIVAL
A Mountain-Bike Mecca

Although it has only been around since 1995, Garda Fest, which takes place for four days in the Italian Alps each spring, is firmly established as the single greatest mountain-bike festival on the planet. Packed with marathon racing, bike exhibitions, stunt riding, music, food and drink, plus plenty of partying, Garda Fest is a splendid celebration of European mountain-bike culture.

The races alone are spectacles to behold. Created by German mountain-bike event pioneer Uli Stanciu, Garda features three impossibly long race courses ranging from 25 to 62 miles (40 to 100 km) that attract more than 2,000 riders each year. The festival also marks the last stop for the arduous eight-day TransAlp race, another brainchild of Stanciu's.

The Garda course itself defines epic. Perched on towering rock edifices, the trails seemingly snake into the sky. The descents are as breathtaking as the panoramic views. And the riding is deliciously rough along paths created hundreds of years ago by shepherds, merchants and military forces. Although the event is in the Alps, which are notorious for cold, wet conditions, the neighbouring Lake Garda helps to moderate temperatures for the festival.

Those who don't wish to race can still ride to their heart's content on the stunning mountain-bike trail system. Exhibitors from around the globe attend, offering cyclists an opportunity to test-drive the best new bikes on the market. The area of Garda Trentino has become a magnet for outdoor enthusiasts both on and off the bike. For some, the highlight of Garda Fest is simply coming together with a few thousand like-minded people to enjoy spectacular natural setting.

Riding ultra-beefy, full-suspension bikes with between 6 and 10 inches (15 to 25 cms) of suspension travel for each wheel and wearing full padding, full-face helmets and baggy shorts and jerseys, experts in the art of freeriding can shred over, jump off or huck themselves across nearly any obstacle, whether man-made or natural. As a reflection of their bravado, freeriders tag their trails, cliffs and gap jumps with grim names such as Lobotomizer 2000 or the Spinal Board.

The freeride crowd has traditionally eschewed any type of organization or competition (a favourite saying is 'bros not pros'), but recently a number of high-profile freeride contests like the Whistler Air Downhill competition in British Columbia, Canada, the Red Bull Rampage in Utah, USA, the Red Bull Downtown (over the streets and staircases) in central Lisbon, Portugal and the race that claims to be the world's toughest, the Red Bull Ride Australia, held at Jindabyne, New South Wales, have gained momentum. Those at the centre of the sport wonder whether competition spells the end of freeriding or just a new incarnation.

In freeriding, *there are no obstacles too great to overcome.*

Bike Counterculture

With roots in both California car culture and Mexican-American culture, lowrider bikes have their own distinct flavour, flare and vision. The preferred basic platform for even the wildest lowrider bike is a Schwinn Sting-Ray frame from the 1960s and 1970s. Customization might include pinstriped candy-coloured paint with glitter, airbrushed fantasy murals, twisted chrome, layers of gold – even hydraulic shocks and booming sound systems bedeck the two-wheeled lowriders that have evolved from bikes to cruising machines evoking the spirits of Jack Nicholson and Dennis Hopper in the film *Easy Rider*.

An everyday sight on the boardwalks of California, lowriders have yet to make an impact in Europe or Australia, although thanks to the enthusiasm of a tiny group of importers, they have begun to appear as props in fashion shoots for cutting-edge style magazines and music videos.

Lowrider bikes are *gold-plated, glitter-encrusted, airbrushed fantasies. In America, lowrider-club members compete with each other to create the most inventive designs.*

ESPN's X Games *has pushed 20-inch riders to new heights and new levels of creativity.*

20-INCH RACING

Action-packed, colourful and highly individualized, the 20-inch bike scene started in southern California in the early 1970s as a way for kids to emulate their heroes on motocross motorcycles and has exploded into a number of factions that include flatland riding (once known as freestyle), street-stunt riding, vertical-ramp riding, 'old school' BMX racing and, in the UK, trials riding.

Thanks in large part to the wildly popular ESPN X Games, broadcast to more than 20 million viewers in 180 countries worldwide, the world of 20-inch bikes has had a recent resurgence in popularity that few could have predicted. Along with the X Games, festivals like the Vans Warped Tour and an endless array of BMX-themed videos and video games feed the demands and desires of the mostly teenage male BMX culture.

DAVE MIRRA
To the Extreme

Mirra has invented *more new tricks and won more big contests than any other BMX rider competing.*

Known as 'Miracle Boy' for his audacious stunt performances, Dave Mirra started competing at 10 and was a sponsored stunt rider by 13. By the time he left school he had turned professional and was considered one of the top ramp riders in the world.

Mirra has earned more medals than anyone in BMX history – 12 X Games medals (9 gold and 3 silver) in street and vert (two 12- to 13-foot [3.6–3.9 m] halfpipe ramps). He was also the first rider to successfully perform a double backflip in competition. *BMX Magazine*

named him Freestyler of the Year in 1999 and ESPN deemed him BMX Rider of the Year in 2001.

Mirra remains one of the most influential athletes in the sport, devoting himself not just to competing, but to developing the sport both in the US and internationally.

VITAL STATS

NATIONALITY: American

DATE OF BIRTH: 4 April 1974

CAREER VICTORY HIGHLIGHTS: Vans Triple Crown: 2001 (3 times) X Games Street: 2000; Gravity Games Vert: 2000; Gravity Games Street: 1999; X Games Street and Vert: 1996, 1997, 1998, 1999

CYCLO-TOURISM

The bicycle means different things to different people, but almost universally the bike stands for freedom and there's no group that embraces the bike-as-freedom concept more than bicycle tourists. Hundreds of thousands of riders log millions of miles every year travelling on every corner of every continent by bicycle.

Tourists range from those who simply strike out on a 25-mile bike-a-thon ride to raise money for a charity to more adventurous souls who load their bikes up with everything they could possibly need for a round-the-world journey. Favoured destinations include the olive-tree-lined roads of Provence, the golden hills of Tuscany, Holland's endless bike paths and the spectacular scenery of the Scottish Highlands. On the other hand, the International Bicycle Fund (IBF) offers a brand of touring that they consider as much a cultural immersion as a two-wheeled holiday. Those on an IBF tour will have off-the-beaten-path experiences in destinations such as Africa, Ecuador, Cuba and Vietnam and will interact with local people and institutions, learning from their culture instead of simply staying in their hotels and eating in their restaurants.

Cycling holidays in the form of fully supported tours covering distances of between 50 and 120 miles (80 to 190 kms) a day, faithful guides and a comfortable hotel room at the day's end are an increasingly popular form of bike touring.

Expansion of the industry has led to greater specialization and there are now tours catering for everyone from vegetarians to Yoga devotees, with routes ranging from sections of the Tour de France to cycling holidays in China.

Ernest Hemingway *wasn't wrong when he said, 'It is by riding a bicycle that you learn the contours of a country best.'*

TANDEMS

Probably the first thing that the Michaux
brothers did after they created their original
boneshaker velocipede was to create a version
of it that they could ride together.

'I think the real appeal of a tandem is that it's another way for a bike
freak to get a two-wheeled fix. It's also a great way for couples – where
the man is usually faster and more into riding – to ride together at the
same speed and have the same great cycling experience. When you're
working well together as a team, an incredible synergy can develop
and that's something that you could never replicate when riding
alone,' comments tandem designer, self-confessed tandem freak
and former bike-shop owner, Scot Nicol of Santa Rosa, California.

When you're working well *together, the intimate synergy of tandem*
riding is an experience you could never match by riding alone.

Tandem riding tends to be a predominantly social activity, enjoyed by couples who often pursue the sport well into old age. A tandem can also be a great way to cycle with children. Many non-cycling groups also use tandems as a means of giving blind people the opportunity to participate in an activity otherwise closed to them.

While there are tandem-only races, the road tandem crowd tends to be more active on the touring and century (100-mile) riding scene. In the UK, tandem races are generally part of road time trials, and the tandems go off at the back of the field. The British Tandem Club organizes both local and national rallies; similar clubs and societies thrive in Holland, Belgium, Germany, France and Austria as well as the USA. International

In the Victorian era, *the tandem was a novel way for two intimates to spend time together.*

rallies held each year in France, Holland and Belgium attract many club members and their families. Tandem riding is increasingly popular in Australia and New Zealand; the Tandem Club of Australia holds a successful annual rally called 'TwoUp', drawing riders from across the country.

Tandems have made incredible advances in lightweight frame, suspension, tyre and disc-brake designs over the past decade. In the US, where off-road conditions are more sympathetic to tandem riding, a large number of off-road tandem rallies have sprung up and tandem categories are now found at the bigger mountain-bike races such as the Sea Otter Classic in Monterey, California, the Leadville Trail 100 in Colorado, and even the challenging 24 Hours of Moab in Utah.

A ride *on a mountain-bike tandem is certain to bring a smile to anyone's face.*

RECUMBENTS

Are recumbent riders unhappy with the traditional bicycle's standing as the most efficient means of transportation in the world (just 35 calories per person per mile as opposed to 1,860 for the average car)? Or are they just people who like to do their own thing? Whatever the case, these fanatics are sensible above all.

The basic form *of the recumbent is the same today as it was in the 1950s. Recumbent designers my have different ideas on geometry, style, look and performance, but for most, the bottom line is comfort.*

Recumbent bikes and their devotees have always been treated as outsiders by the main cycling community. When the recumbent bike – defined as any bicycle that you ride in a prone position – was banned by the UCI in 1934 after an early recumbent design was used to smash many world records, recumbent riders were forced to create their own clubs, events and organizing body, the International Human Powered Vehicle Association (IHPVA).

Around the middle of the 20th century, the recumbent world was a very quiet and lonely place to be, but in the early 1980s, when the E. I. Dupont company offered $15,000 to the first human-powered machine that could break 65 miles per hour, the cult of the recumbent regenerated. Today you can find recumbent-centric clubs and groups in a growing number of countries, including the UK, France, Belgium, Holland, the US and Australia.

An upright position, *comfortable saddle, streamlined aerodynamics and steady handling geometry all characterize the recumbent bike.*

CHARITY RIDES

Organized rides satisfy many needs and wants for cyclists – community, camaraderie, challenge, a sense of purpose and the chance for social activism. Add to this the satisfaction of raising money for a good cause and it is easy to see why charity rides have become popular all over the world.

The methods employed to generate funds vary enormously, ranging from the individual, such as Englishman Alastair Humphreys, currently cycling solo 70,000 miles (112,630 km) around the world to raise money for a children's charity, to organized group activities such as the popular 56-mile (90-km) London to Brighton ride in Britain, that attracted around 27,000 participants in 2003. Charity

The AIDS/LifeCycle *ride from San Francisco to Los Angeles in the US raises millions of dollars every year.*

rides can bring together interesting groups of people for maximum publicity, such as Pollie Pedal in Australia, an annual cycle ride (begun in 2000), encouraging politicians to ride their bikes to raise money for charity and awareness of key issues.

One of the earliest and best-known charity cycling movements originated in San Francisco in 1994 to raise funds and awareness of AIDS. Now billed as 'The AIDS/LifeCycle', the 585-mile (940-km) ride from San Francisco to Los Angeles attracts more than 900 riders and raises millions for the San Francisco AIDS Foundation and the LA Gay and Lesbian Center every June. The format has been copied around the United States and now multi-day tours that benefit HIV/AIDS research or charities are held every summer across the country.

As AIDS became the biggest worldwide medical issue in the 1990s, eclipsing even bigger threats like heart disease and cancer, the AIDS Rides grew. Thousands of people – many of them complete cycling novices who generally rode only short distances – were riding hundreds of miles in five, six and seven days to raise millions of dollars for research for a cure.

If the effect on the research community was huge, it had no less impact on the riders, many of whom were attracted to the rides because of friends and loved ones lost to the devastating effects of AIDS.

Crossing finish lines in countless cities across the country, grown men and women collapsed and cried, not from pain or exhaustion, but from overpowering emotion – the feeling that in the face of a faceless killer that could not be stopped, they were doing *something*, that somehow they were helping.

Riders celebrate *their accomplishment, a familiar sight since the first AIDS ride in 1994.*

A TOOL IN THE WORKPLACE

There may always be hot debate about who actually invented the bike, whether it was the French, the English, or even the Chinese, but one thing is for sure: long before it was raced over the roads of France, the bike was used as a tool in the workplaces of the world.

Once the industrial revolution was in full swing, the bike-as-tool was a common sight and it wasn't until the car reached critical mass that the bike was outdone for convenience and utility.

The Tour de France *would be a piece of cake compared to pedalling up a hill with this load.*

The original US Postal Service *cycling team, wool uniforms and all.*

A Nation on Wheels

The simple, unadorned bicycle is a symbol as evocative of China as the Great Wall itself. For decades, the 'steel horse' has been the primary means of transportation for the average Chinese citizen to negotiate dusty city streets on the way to work, run errands and attend leisure activities. Unlike the great serpentine barrier, the bicycle may soon all but recede from view in a nation where it once ruled.

China's love affair with bicycles began in the late 19th century, when Americans Thomas Gaskell Allen Jr and William Lewis Sachtleben spent two years pedalling the 7,000 miles (11,260 km) from Constantinople to Peking. Villagers met them with enthusiastic fervour and before long, Chinese royalty had taken a fancy to two-wheeling around the palace grounds.

Following the 1949 Communist Revolution, a mass bicycle movement emerged, when the government encouraged – and actually subsidized – families to purchase bicycles. As China opened up economically during the decades that followed, bike ownership soared.

Today, a rapidly growing number of citizens are interested in 'upgrading' their two-wheeled vehicles to the four-wheeled variety. Cars are the new status symbol in a nation keen to modernize – a development that is causing unprecedented traffic snarl-ups. As pollution and traffic jams increase, trips via bicycle have fallen dramatically. The one-time bicycle epicentre of Shanghai has plans to force bicycles out by 2010.

MESSENGERS

Facing danger, catastrophe and contempt down every avenue, the life of a bike messenger is one of absolute extremes. Often underpaid and always under-insured, they are a tight-knit group that, while even in fierce competition for the most lucrative runs, maintains an intense loyalty to their brotherhood. The generally poor working conditions and knowledge that tomorrow could be their last day, have led to the formation of a number of umbrella groups or associations that give the independent messengers some collective leverage when it comes to bargaining for wages, improving working conditions or upgrading equipment.

With a cab *and a courier in quarters this close, an altercation is sure to follow.*

Perhaps looking to recreate the thrill of their hours on the clock, messengers are increasingly using their leisure time for bike-oriented events from weekly rides and weekend tours to the illegal Alleycat races popular in the US, in which messengers pit their skill and daring against city streets filled with traffic. Every year the messengers of the world select an urban setting for the Messenger World Championships. Proof of the global reach of the two-wheeled messenger, the competition has been held in Seattle (USA, 2003), Copenhagen (Denmark, 2002), Budapest (Hungary, 2001), Philadelphia (USA, 2000) and Zurich (Switzerland, 1999), with future venues including Mexico City (proposed for 2005). Partly a race, definitely a party, the Messenger World Championships event is hard to beat when it comes to fun and freakishness.

A trio of messengers *battle it out at the annual Cycle Messenger World Championships.*

MOUNTED POLICE

Detroit, Michigan, was one of the first cities in the United States to employ the bicycle in the fight against crime when in 1897 expert cyclists called 'Scorchers' were used to stop speeding cyclists in the pre-car city.

Around that time, the local policeman on his bicycle was a common sight in Britain's rural towns and villages. Only recently have police developed the use of mountain-bike patrols, with pilot schemes such as the city of York's Community Cycle Unit reporting excellent results. Four officers have been trained to patrol on Scott mountain bikes, specially equipped with blue flashing lights and sirens. The bikes have proved effective in responding to incidents in pedestrianized areas and, unlike police cars, are not subject

An early company *of Scorchers muster for inspection.*

(left) Cycling over the Golden Gate *Bridge on a sunny day seems like a fine way to do policework.*

(right) Four mounted police *stand ready at a protest.*

to inner-city traffic. Thanks to the benefits of daily exercise, the York team had an unbroken attendance record during the pilot period. More importantly, data showed that the bike police arrested 45% more offenders than other local officers. Results such as these make it highly likely that the police officer on a bicycle will once again be commonplace in villages, towns and cities across the UK.

In Australia, as in America, mountain bikes have become increasingly popular over the years, and are now recognized as an effective and efficient policing tool. Factors of stealth, approachability by the public, manoeuvrability, cost-saving and officer work satisfaction have all made the bikes a huge success.

Cycle-mounted military units *were used by the Germans in World War II. In this photo from 1940, bicycle-mounted German soldiers enter a Norwegian port.*

ARMY

The Chinese army is said to have used a rudimentary 'walking machine' to send messages between troop formations as early as 1810. Later in the 19th century, England, France and Switzerland among others had complete bicycle-mounted corps; in fact, Switzerland maintained a large bicycle-mounted unit until very recently.

The 25th Infantry Bicycle Corps, a unit of the Buffalo Soldiers, was America's first bicycle-mounted unit; noteworthy both for the mode of transportation and because all of its members were of African-American descent. In a legendary escapade in 1897, the 25th, looking to demonstrate the bicycle's effectiveness as a troop transport, rode 1,900 miles (3,057 km) from their base in Montana to Saint Louis, Missouri. As a reward for their ingenuity, the Buffalo Soldiers of the 25th were sent to Cuba to keep peace in Havana in the wake of the Spanish-American war.

The British ceased to use bicycles after World War I, as it was found to be difficult to keep hold of them in enemy territory. The Americans, however, persevered and in World War II entire units of specially trained paratroopers were dropped into battle with custom folding bicycles strapped to their packs.

In recent years, advances in bike technology have again given the bicycle currency with the world's armed forces.

The Belgian Congo *cyclist company, active during World War II.*

FAUSTO COPPI
Symbol of a Rising Nation

Fausto Coppi may not be the greatest cyclist who ever lived, but he accomplished one of the greatest feats an athlete can – elevating his countrymen during their darkest hours. As an army infantryman in Tortona, Coppi rose to cycling prominence during the 1940s and 1950s, at a time when Italy was recovering from the devastation of World War I and years spent toiling under a dictatorship. As the unofficial ambassador of the nation, the *Campionissimo* (the Great Champion) represented a resurgent spirit in the population.

Coppi was easily the best time triallist of his day. So electrifying were his performances in the mountains that he won the 1952 Tour de France by a stunning 29 minutes and wasn't invited back the following year for fear that he would dominate again. His duels with arch rival and fellow Italian Gino Bartali are legendary.

Equally legendary is how Coppi met his demise. A series of unfortunate events including his brother's death in a crash in 1951 and an illicit love affair with a married woman (he, too, was married) in 1953 detracted from his performance. Then in 1959, during a trip to Africa for an exhibition race, Coppi caught malaria. The disease was misdiagnosed and he died in Italy aged 40. More than 40 years later, Italian prosecutors reopened the case, claiming they had evidence that the great Coppi had been poisoned by a rival in Africa. The allegations have been largely dismissed, but the Italian legend's death will nonetheless always be a mystery.

VITAL STATS

NATIONALITY: Italian

DATE OF BIRTH: 15 September 1919

CAREER VICTORY HIGHLIGHTS: Tour de France: 1949, 1952; Giro d'Italia: 1940, 1947, 1949, 1952, 1953; Milan–San Remo: 1946, 1948, 1949; Paris–Roubaix: 1950; World Hour Record: 1942

BIKE ADVOCATES

With a dream of making their cities
and streets more livable and safe, bicycle
advocates fight to make the bike a broadly
accepted mode of everyday transport.

Pro-active bicycle campaigners *Chris Carlsson* (left) *and colleague Jim Swanson.*

On the last Friday of September in 1992, American bike advocates staged their most high-profile, high-impact escapade, gathering en masse in the streets of San Francisco at the height of the Friday rush hour in order to demonstrate the very real effect that the bicycle can have on traffic. Led by sometime bike messenger, writer and local historian Chris Carlsson and a few friends, the group spun the mantra 'We're not blocking traffic, we are traffic', into a monthly traffic jam and a radical mission to give 'bicyclists of all persuasions the chance to see that we are not alone and that we, too, have a right to the road'.

Less of an organized movement than an 'unorganized coincidence', like-minded cyclists have formed Critical Mass groups in cities across the globe. The first London Critical Mass happened in April 1994 with a group of around 50 cyclists; subsequent summer masses have been known to attract well over a thousand. As in most cities, rides take place once a month, with a designated rally point for the start.

Different Masses may take on concerns specific to the city they happen in, but overall Critical Mass has successfully advocated bike-friendly issues such as bike lanes, bike racks on buses, car-free zones and improved public transport in dozens of cities around the world.

The popularity *of the high-wheeler peaked in 1880, but enthusiasts, like this American group, still abound.*

CHAPTER 3

HISTORY

By Joe Lindsey

MAN-MADE MACHINE

The inventions that change the world
are often those that carry the most sublime
versatility, a seamless transfer from one use to
the next. The bicycle is one such invention. It
is simultaneously transportation, recreation,
freedom and mobility.

Bicycles are used to ferry goods, to travel long distances quickly
and efficiently and to open new opportunities. Bicycles are affordable
to most of the world's population; for many, they are the primary
means of transportation after walking. Bikes are cheaper to own
than horses or cars, easier to store and more efficient per mile
than any other form of transportation ever invented. And
they've captivated our imaginations for centuries.

(continued on page 127)

Practical additions such
*as the basket and rear
rack make the bicycle
sublimely versatile.*

An early *freerider catches a lift.*

Workers in Asia *give a first-hand lesson on the versatility and cost effectiveness of the bicycle.*

Army cadets *at the Royal Military Academy Sandhurst (Sussex, England) line up with their bikes in this photo from 1927.*

The first known drawing of a bicycle-like machine can be found in Leonardo da Vinci's *Codex Atlanticus*, a collection of manuscript sheets from Leonardo's original notebooks containing studies and drawings dating from around 1493 (and which also featured a drawing resembling a hang-glider). While the actual bicycle design is thought to have come from an apprentice of his (see page 187), da Vinci also sketched a chain-and-cog drive mechanism and even ball bearings in other notebooks, inventions that would not surface for more than 400 years but which would have immense impact not only on the bicycle but also on the dawn of the Industrial Revolution.

This child is fascinated *by a wooden model of Leonardo's early design.*

Two-wheeled devices that rolled under human power wouldn't really come into existence until the early 18th century. The earliest known is the Laufmaschine (or 'running machine'), also known as the 'Draisienne' (after its inventor) or the 'swiftwalker', which was first demonstrated in August 1817. It was certainly primitive – a wooden beam set between two wheels – but it had a steering mechanism and a seat and looked, actually, not too far removed from a modern recumbent bike.

The Laufmaschine was an intriguing invention, but its central limitation was its speed under human power. Inventor Karl von Drais claimed in his patent application that on level ground the machine was capable of going 9 miles (14.5 km) an hour; faster than walking to be sure, but far below even a tourist's pace on a modern bike today. The problem was drive – you pushed off the

(continued on page 131)

Von Drais's *Laufmaschine was all the rage in Paris in 1817.*

By the 1870s
*the Laufmaschine
had evolved into
the Michaux-style
velocipede seen here.*

THE BICYCLE SEAT
The Pedaller's Perch

Throughout history, the bicycle seat has taken quite a bum rap. Sore-bottomed critics have blamed the humble saddle for everything from boils to impotence. The quest for a more comfortable ride has led inventors to concoct saddles resembling everything from a toilet seat to a hammock,

eventually settling into the popular bike seat of today – an amalgamation of the rest. Possibly recognizing the need to relieve pressure on delicate tissues, early saddles of the late 1800s were part doughnut, part commode. The popular Bunker Pneumatic design of 1892 resembled a modern comfort saddle, except that it was hollowed out in the region of the buttock and crotch. The Safety Poise Pneumatic of 1898 was shaped less like a saddle and more like an inner tube, providing only a circle of support to sit on.

Tinkerers continued adjusting the design, at one point developing a split saddle that allowed each half to move independently as the rider pedalled. In 1966, inventor Dan Henry attached an upside-down set of drop bars where the saddle should be with fabric slung between the two bar ends to make a

riding hammock – doubtless comfortable for sitting, but none too safe for riding. The saddle craze settled down soon after that, with most seats resembling the classic shape we know today: long, slender nose and flared back.

Then in the mid-1990s, controversy rolled into the saddle industry again, this time on the back of some well-publicized research that bike seats caused impotency. Offended racers paraded out their children to refute this, but the bike industry quickly designed 'anatomically correct' saddles with small grooves or cut outs in the nose to relieve unwanted pressure. So the story ends – for now.

In the past 150 years, *saddles have progressed from early torture devices to ultra-comfortable gel-injected seats.*

ground on the Laufmaschine rather than pedalling and so at maximum speed, the rider couldn't get any more purchase – it was terminal velocity. Two Scotsmen, Kirkpatrick MacMillan and Gavin Dalzell, working nearly simultaneously, are credited with adding mechanical drive to the 'velocipede', as the early bicycle was called. Hand and foot treadle cranks were both tried, with limited success; MacMillan never patented his invention, nor did it ever go into production. The beginnings of the real bicycle, that pedal-driven invention we are familiar with – from the quaint solid-rubber-tyred high-wheeler to the modern downhill bike with 9 inches (23 cms) of suspension travel and hydraulic disc brakes – had to wait until the 1860s. *(continued on page 136)*

EVOLUTION OF THE BICYCLE

1817 LAUFMASCHINE

1871 HIGH-WHEELER

1896 RECUMBENT

1938 SCHWINN EXCELSIOR OR CRUISER

1863 PEDAL VELOCIPEDE

1884 HARD-TYRED SAFETY

1933 SCHWINN AEROCYCLE

1946

BOWDEN SPACELANDER

1963

SCHWINN STING-RAY

1977

MOUNTAIN BIKE

2004

TREK 1500

1951

CAMPAGNOLO GRAN
SPORT DERAILLEUR

1970

BMX BIKE

1982

SPECIALIZED STUMPJUMPER OR
UNIVEGA ALPINO PRO

Hell of the North

The beauty of Paris–Roubaix is that it exists. Most agree that a race so treacherous couldn't be designed today. After all, what pro roadie would want to risk bent wheels and broken limbs in the dangerous inferno of crashes that plague a race so wicked that it's been deemed the 'Hell of the North'? Yet nearly 200 of the top riders in the world show up each year for this gruelling century-old challenge that now makes up one of the 10 UCI World Cup races (see page 165). Originally designed in 1896 as a warm-up for the Bordeaux–Paris race, Paris–Roubaix has developed a fervent following among racers and fans alike. Also known as the 'Queen of

The Queen of the Classics, *Paris–Roubaix has always been a gritty and demanding race.*

the Classics', the course snakes 170 miles (270 km) through the narrow, rough roads from Paris to Roubaix, a small town on the Belgian border. What sets it apart from other single-day European classics is the *pavé*, some 30 miles (50 km) of cobbled tracks that pummel what little energy is left out of already weary racers. As if the merciless terrain were not enough, Paris–Roubaix is equally notorious for its impossible racing conditions. Held close to Easter each year, the weather tends to be rainy and damp, making negotiating the *pavé* sections akin to biking on ice. Dry weather is little better, as hundreds of wheels kick up dark brown clouds of choking dust. Through the years, as more *pavé* roads have become paved roads, the race has been re-routed to maintain its rugged difficulty.

The result: no race beside the Tour de France boasts such an illustrious list of victors, including Fausto Coppi, Eddy Merckx and Bernard Hinault. Often, there is one lone rider who survives the cobbles and pulls into the Roubaix velodrome for a victory lap well ahead of his fellow contenders, basking in some well-deserved limelight. Ever since its inception, a win in Roubaix is truly a badge of honour.

Bumping along *the* pavé *is par for the course during this 170-mile (270-km) challenge.*

BIRTH OF THE BICYCLE

Like many inventions – the television, for example – the identity of the bicycle's true inventor is somewhat up for debate and the inventions that popularized it – pneumatic tyres, gear differentials and suspension – were the contributions of many different people.

The father-son team of Pierre and Ernest Michaux are commonly credited with 'inventing' the bicycle in 1864 at their Parisian carriage shop. It's unknown which member of the Michaux family had the idea to put pedal cranks on a velocipede, but the invention was a quantum leap

A Michaux velocipede
dating from 1869.

for the nascent bicycle. Quantum in the physics sense: there was no historical basis for a pedal crank for propulsion; the idea was truly original.

Why is a pedal crank so significant? A treadle crank, in which a lever arm is drawn back and forth like an oar to create torque, is limited by the rate of that back-and-forth motion; one can only row so fast. But pedal cranks spin in a circle, meaning that the pedaller never has to reverse the momentum at the end of the power stroke; power is also delivered more consistently (levelling out the peaks and dead spots in a treadle stroke) and rapidly, allowing average speeds that dwarfed the top speed of the swiftwalker or a treadle-crank machine.

Attaching a lever *arm directly to a wheel completed the basic structure of the bicycle.*

Also laying some claim to the bicycle's invention was Frenchman Pierre Lallement, who holds the first known patent on a bicycle, dated 20 November 1866. Lallement had worked for the Michauxs around 1865 but claimed in his patent that his invention dated from an idea he'd had in 1862 and that he'd built his first bicycle, or 'pedal velocipede', as they were then known, in 1863.

(right) Pierre Lallement, *who was employed by the Michauxs in 1865, held the first-known patent for a bicycle, dated 1863.*

(facing page) A detail *of the early pedal crank.*

The French were the early world leaders in bicycle design, with innovations such as the metal-spoked wheel, a four-speed gear, and a freewheel featured at the Paris Velocipede Exhibition of 1869. However, the nascent industry suffered a severe setback with the advent of the Franco-Prussian war of 1870. Fortunately, the passion for velocipedes had spread beyond the borders of France and development continued elsewhere. Lallement had taken his prototype to America, and his patent was an American one that was to

By 1869, *Lallement's patented velocipede was sold throughout America. This illustration is taken from an advertising flyer for his invention.*

This early rail bike *could be pedalled and cranked anywhere there were tracks.*

Whimsy and innovation *were common themes in early-20th-century Art Nouveau bicycle advertisements (see Chapter 4).*

change hands several times. The fight over royalties and subsequent consolidation of the bicycle industry were parts of the zeitgeist that ushered in the Gilded Age of American bicycle manufacture; at one point the monolithic American Bicycle Company (ABC) had John D. Rockefeller as one of its controlling partners. In England, meanwhile, a strong bicycle manufacturing trade developed in the industrial Midlands, particularly around Coventry.

Innovation continued with the invention of the ball-bearing, patented in the 1860s. Metal roller and ball bearings replaced primitive and temperamental sleeve bushings made of materials such as leather and wood. The incredible decrease in friction allowed longer durability of any wheeled contrivance,

A wise husband *will always give his mother-in-law the best bike.*

whether a bicycle or industrial implement, and represented a considerable advance.

As much as friction and durability of the hub parts, the central problem of the early bicycle was its direct drive; the only way to get a higher gear was to build a larger driving wheel. The high-wheelers that developed in the late 19th century had front wheels ranging from 50 to 60 inches (127 to 152 cms) in diameter – nearly 5-feet (1.5-m) tall. In Britain, the nickname 'penny-farthing' was given as the size of the wheels resembled the difference between a penny and a farthing coin. The rider was perched on a simple serpentine-style frame bar above the front wheel – a precarious position given the twitchy handling and bumpy ride.

Nineteenth-century *high-wheeler-mounted deliverymen enjoy a respite from their rounds.*

In the early days *of the car both high-wheeler and 'safety' bicycles were a common sight on the streets.*

Furthermore, gear size was somewhat limited by rider size (the length of the rider's leg had to be at least half that of the wheel diameter or he couldn't reach the pedals). Braking was dangerous at best – an arm-driven lever was depressed on the front tyre – but the so-called spoon brake did little to slow the bike, nor would you want it to be especially powerful or an over-the-bars trip might ensue. Riders more commonly slowed the bike by applying back pressure on the pedals.

A dapper young gentleman *on a particularly ornate Michaux-era 'boneshaker' velocipede.*

Cycle racing *in its earliest form, from around the 1870s.*

The size of *a high-wheeler could sometimes be advantageous.*

Various high-wheel makers experimented with chain drives; the earliest we know of is Frenchmen Ernest Meyer and André Guilmet's chain-and-cog system in 1868; their invention never took hold, though and it was up to later cycle makers such as English manufacturer Thomas Humber, who first adapted chain-and-cog setups from machinery to bicycle use.

Despite their problems, high-wheel bicycles were still preferable to 'safeties', bicycles with more or less equally sized wheels, because of one additional factor that ranks above raw speed: comfort.

(left) This safety *has variable gearing.*

(right) An early *safety is carefully inspected.*

After nearly *half a century of experimentation, the modern safety bicycle became what we know today as a bicycle.*

The solid rubber tyres then available afforded a harsh and bumpy ride and the larger wheels of the so-called 'ordinaries' (as the high-wheelers were then known, to differentiate them from the 'safeties') were more adept at absorbing impact through the spokes. This became particularly true when English inventor James Starley pioneered the use of tangentially spoked wheels, where the spokes leave the hub at an angle and cross over other spokes. The design, first used in the 1880s, was so good that it is still the primary spoke pattern today. Starley, a prescient man with a gift for engineering, also gave us hollow frame tubing and an invention that would eventually find its greatest use in the car: differential gears allowing two wheels on the same axle to turn at different rates.

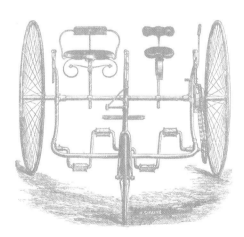

James Starley *also built this side-by-side 'sociable' cycle, while his workshop perfected his safety bicycle.*

Three owners of *high-wheelers stand proudly beside their machines.*

The differential is the basis for controlling any vehicle with multi-track wheels.

But another innovation vied for the unofficial title of most wide-reaching: the pneumatic tyre. In 1888, John Boyd Dunlop, a Scottish veterinarian, living in Belfast, Northern Ireland, was trying to give his son's tricycle a smoother ride when he hit upon the idea of using air to cushion the ride. He took thin sheets of rubber and wrapped them around the wheels, gluing them together to form a continuous layer and inflated them with a football pump. Intuitively sensing the impact of his then-crude invention, Dunlop applied for a patent later that year.

The tyres were an instant hit, were sold in most of the Western world by the turn of the century and instantly revolutionized bike design by making the ride more comfortable. Bikes with smaller wheels could now roll over many obstacles. The ride wasn't so harsh as to merit the derisive nickname 'boneshaker', which had been given to early velocipedes; when the tyres were combined with the chain-driven drivetrain, safety bikes became an obvious choice over high-wheel models.

A side effect of the pneumatic tyre was the creation of better brakes – the weak spoon-lever-type brake didn't work as well on pneumatic tyres. The higher speeds achievable with air-filled tyres also necessitated stronger brakes, which resulted in the first coaster-brake hub (the 'New Departure', in 1898) and the caliper rim brakes we know today. Dunlop's invention also spurred the first freewheel, which was

In 1888 John Boyd Dunlop invented the pneumatic air tyre in order to cushion the ride of his son's bicycle.

The great advantage *of pneumatic tyres was that their air cushioning allowed for wheels to be made smaller – signalling the end of the high-wheeler.*

Looking similar to *the bicycles of today, this late-19th-century Humber has a diamond safety frame, rear suspension, pneumatic tyres and lever-activated brakes*

introduced in 1897 and allowed riders to coast at speeds faster than they could pedal.

By the turn of the 19th century, many of the basic components of the modern bicycle had been introduced, if not perfected. However, the period marked the end of cycling's golden age as the advent of the automobile had a profound influence on the role of the bicycle in society. In large countries such as America and Australia, where great distances were the norm, the enthusiasm for the bicycle that had characterized the late 19th century was quickly transferred to the new method of transport. In Europe, however, particularly during the hardships suffered throughout the two World Wars, the bicycle continued to be a useful and cost-effective way to travel, and cycling both as a recreational pastime and a general means of transportation expanded in parallel with the development of the car.

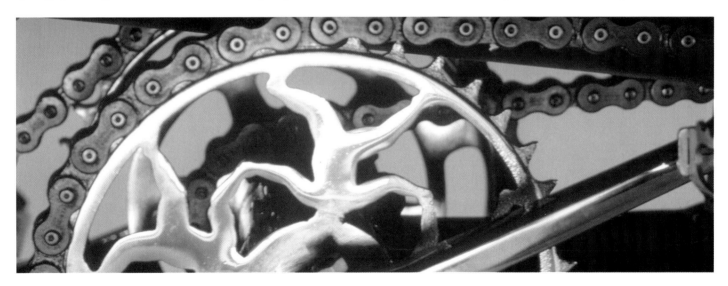

The Best There Ever Was

Put Lance Armstrong, Greg LeMond, Miguel Indurain and Fausto Coppi in a room and they will stand in the shadow of a giant who will probably never be surpassed – Eddy Merckx. 'The Cannibal', as he was known, for his insatiable appetite to win, collected 525 victories, including five Tours de France, during his astonishing 14-year career.

What sets Merckx apart is the sheer scope of his ability. He wasn't just a Tour rider or a Classics man; he won everything – single-day events, stage races, long tours and hour-long efforts. He competed in 1,800 races and captured a record 34 stages of the Tour de France. During his first Tour, he finished 18 minutes ahead and had worn all three

Eddy! Eddy! Eddy! Allez Eddy! *Merckx is cheered on by a trio of enthusiastic spectators.*

leaders' jerseys for overall champion, king of the mountain and points winner.

Eventually, of course, the great Cannibal would lose his teeth. His gruelling schedule compounded by lingering injuries from crashes took their toll in 1975, when Merckx was vying for an unprecedented sixth Tour de France victory. He could no longer dominate the mountains or excel in the time trials. He came in second that year to Bernard Thevenet and retired three years later at the age of 32.

Today, Merckx is often on hand to watch races, and lends his keen building expertise to his namesake line of professional-calibre racing bikes.

VITAL STATS

NATIONALITY: Belgian

DATE OF BIRTH: 17 June 1945

CAREER VICTORY HIGHLIGHTS:

Tour de France: 1969, 1970, 1971, 1972, 1974

Giro d'Italia: 1968, 1972, 1973, 1974

Milan–San Remo: 1966, 1967, 1969, 1971, 1972, 1975, 1976

Paris–Roubaix: 1968, 1970, 1973

World Hour Record: 1972

NEW DEVELOPMENTS

The Great Depression (1930–40) forced many American cycle makers to shut their doors. In 1933, one of the few that remained trading, Arnold, Schwinn & Co., introduced a seemingly insignificant tyre size that would revolutionize the bike industry.

Called the 'balloon tyre' for its fat casing and soft, bouncy ride, the new tyre was 26 by 2.125 inches (66 by 5.4 cm). Its invention was quickly followed by a succession of cruisers, complete with cantilevered frame designs, faux petrol tanks and backswept handlebars. The most notable of these was the 1938 Excelsior,

Not quite what *Ignaz Schwinn had in mind, but this Depression-era dreamer had the right idea.*

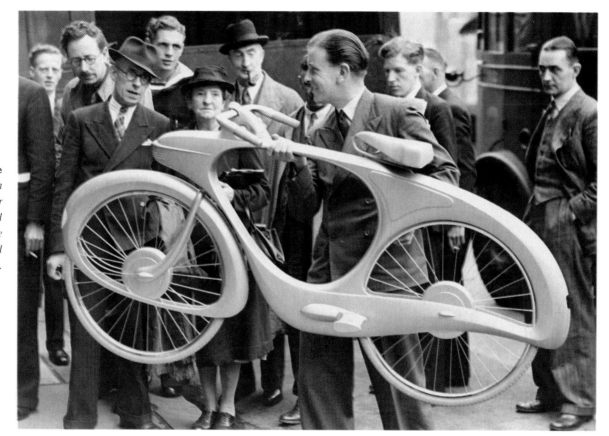

An early prototype *of the Bowden Spacelander. Just over 500 of the original working models were ever produced and fewer than 50 remain.*

The invention of Campagnolo's *cable-actuated rear derailleur was a significant advance in the development of the modern racing bike.*

which four decades later would become the chassis for the mountain bike.

Other significant developments in the US involved artistic approaches to the bike that produced beautiful, futuristic oddities like 1946's legendary Bowden Spacelander (pictured page 159).

Of the more practical inventions, the most interesting was probably the modern parallelogram derailleur, the Campagnolo Gran Sport, in 1951. The Gran Sport was preceded by a number of crude gear-changing mechanisms, from the Chemineau of 1911 to the Simplex Tour de France derailleur of the 1930s. Derailleur development was hindered in part by racing, as the Tour de France did not allow derailleurs until 1929, requiring riders to dismount and flip the wheel between the freewheel mounted on each side – the venerable 'flip-flop' hub.

Italian rider Tullio Campagnolo, who essentially invented the modern derailleur, also conceived the quick-release, tools-free wheel skewer after a hellish moment in the 1927 Gran Premio della Vittoria race when the wing nuts on his front wheel froze as he tried to remove it for a tyre change in the bitter cold of the Dolomites.

The refinement from the drop parallelogram to the slant parallelogram helped pave the way for modern indexed shifting.

Campagnolo *on the Croce d'Aune Pass in 1927 – a blustery snow-filled day that would result in an historic innovation.*

THE MODERN AGE

In the early 1970s, a number of cyclists in the San Francisco area took an interest in old Schwinn balloon-tyre cruisers, in particular, the sturdy 1938 Excelsior, which became the test chassis for many of their experiments. The balloon tyre's considerable width and volume made it aptly suited for riding off-road.

The earliest protagonists were the Cupertino Riders, a loosely knit band of 10 cyclists who delighted in racing fat-tyre cruisers down the fire roads of the surrounding California coast range. On 1 December, 1974, three of the group (who also went by the name of the 'Morrow Dirt Club' for the Morrow coaster brake that they used) entered the West Coast Open Cyclo-Cross Championships – a tiny event of a niche sport that would nonetheless be groundbreaking in its aftermath.

The Cupertino Riders *are said to have been the first to tack a rear derailleur on to a fat-tyre bike.*

The Open Championships were aptly named because any rider could ride any bike, as opposed to the normal rigour of categories and strict rules that determined which bikes were acceptable. Russ Mahon, leader of the Cupertino group, rode a 1930s cruiser brake with derailleurs grafted onto the frame and motorcycle-style drum brakes. Also racing that day (on conventional cyclo-cross bikes) were Joe Breeze, Charlie Kelly and Gary Fisher, who were also experimenting with riding cruisers off-road. Mahon, unknowingly, contributed hugely to the nascent collective consciousness of what would become mountain biking: by adding gears, he made it possible to ride up the hills as well as down. Breeze, Kelly and Fisher were already riding down mountain trails in their Marin County home – a pursuit that would soon be immortalized in the first-known

Marin County, *California's Charlie Kelly, an early chronicler of the fat-tyre scene.*

Gary 'Pops' Fisher, *one of mountain biking's greatest proponents and personalities.*

Single-Day Sensations

World Cup winners are the one-hit wonders of the cycling community. Most don't have the elite physical prowess to dominate a gruelling three-week Tour. But on any given race day, they can fight for the line with the best and the brightest. And the one racer who shines the brightest throughout the season gets the big pot of gold – and a rainbow jersey – at the end.

The World Cup races are a series of 10 single-day events. The series itself is relatively new, first kicking off in 1989 (although it long-existed as the Pernod Super Prestige Trophy). Though the individual races are not as long as the great Tours, they are equally spectacular and often punishing. Like the Tours, the World Cup events are exclusively European. They include esteemed, century-old classic races such as Liège–Bastogne–Liège, which winds more than 150 miles (240 km) through rugged Belgian countryside; the bone-chattering Paris–Roubaix; Italy's magnificent Milan–San Remo and Giro di Lombardia; Spain's San Sebastian; and relative newcomer the Netherlands' demanding Amstel Gold. Top-finishing racers earn points in each event; a white jersey bearing the world champion rainbow stripes is awarded to the ultimate winner.

The mountain-bike World Cup championship series consists of eight events that take over 150 top-class men and women around the globe to various, ever-changing locales, including Hungary, Portugal, Germany and the UK. The World Cup is considered one of the three most prestigious off-road titles, the other two being the NORBA (National Off-Road Bicycle Association) national series and the Olympics.

Recent winners include Belgium's Johan Museeuw, Germany's Erik Zabel and Alison Dunlap of the United States (off-road).

Winners of the women's *World Cup downhill race (Kaprun, Austria) celebrate on the podium.*

mountain-bike race – the legendary Repack Downhill down Mount Tamalpais in Marin County. Mahon's invention meant that they could ride to places without having to push their bikes up the hills.

Gary Fisher put Mahon's ideas to work in 1976 on his own bike and for years he was widely credited with the invention of the mountain bike. Fisher, along with Charlie Kelly and Tom Ritchey, did create the first

company devoted to producing mountain bikes and even attempted to patent the term 'mountain bike'. But truth be told, the mountain bike, much as the original bicycle itself, was the result of several different isolated inventors, such as Mahon, Fisher and others, contributing various essential parts of the equation to create something that far surpassed the sum of the individual pieces.

One seminal creator was Joe Breeze, a frame builder who in 1977 crafted the first real mountain bike, a hand-made frame constructed with all-new components specifically for the purpose of riding off-road. 'The Breezer', as his creation was called, had a chrome-moly steel frame, Simplex touring derailleurs, triple crankset, cantilever brakes and wide knobby tyres. Breeze produced just

(continued on page 170)

Few have done *as much to evolve the bicycle and people's attitudes towards it as Joe Breeze, seen here racing down Repack in the late 1970s.*

JEANNIE LONGO
An Enduring Pioneer

Though physically a diminutive 5-foot, 2-inch (1.58-m), 102-pound (46-kg) woman, Jeannie Longo is a cyclist of superior strength and indomitable spirit. Taking to the bike during an era when the male-dominated sport frowned on female competitors, Longo smashed through gender barriers and broke records for a remarkable quarter of a century.

A natural athlete, Longo grew up hiking, swimming, skiing and cycling. In 1979, she decided to aim for the 1980 World Cycling Championships simply because they were taking place in her home town of Sallanches, in the Haute-Savoie region of France. To qualify, she got her licence and jumped into the French Championships, which she soundly won aged only 21. Supremely confident and street-fighter tough, Longo

has a reputation for being a volatile rebel, often battling with team-mates, sponsors and the media. Once she was almost disqualified from the World Championships for refusing to wear her sponsor's shoes. But even those who dislike her style cannot argue with her substance. Longo has racked up an

astonishing 710 career wins – more than any other cyclist, male or female, in history. She has 46 National Championship titles, 3 women's Tour de France victories and a drawerful of Olympic medals. Her longevity in the sport is equally unprecedented. In 1996, Longo took gold

VITAL STATS

NATIONALITY: French

DATE OF BIRTH: 31 October 1958

CAREER VICTORY HIGHLIGHTS: Tour de France: 1987, 1988, 1989; Olympic Road: 1996; World Champion: 1985, 1986, 1987, 1988, 1989, 1995, 1996, 1997, 2001; World Hour Record: 1995, 1996; French Champion: 1979, 1980, 1981, 1982, 1983, 1984, 1985, 1986, 1987, 1988, 1989, 1992, 1995

and silver in the Olympic Games in Atlanta and beat the world hour record. She also turned 38 years old. Now in her mid-40s, she still does not talk of retirement. She credits her staying power to her mental toughness and meticulous organic diet. Love her or hate her, Longo is an icon the sport will not soon forget.

Jeannie Longo *is probably the most successful professional cyclist in history.*

10 bikes for himself and some like-minded friends, but by the time number 10 was done, orders from interested riders began to trickle in.

Ritchey was the sport's first prolific builder, crafting hundreds of frames for Fisher and Kelly's 'Fisher MountainBikes' (sic) company. The three later went their separate ways, but in 1979 Kelly published an article on the innovative sport in *Outside* magazine and the word was out. In 1982 the first mass-produced mountain bikes, the Specialized Stumpjumper and the Univega Alpina Pro, were unveiled. They were the first widely sold and affordable mountain bikes in existence and an acquisitive, interested riding public snapped them up. The resultant boom echoed the original *velocipedomania* with thousands of people worldwide jumping into the newly created sport. In just two short decades, mountain biking went from an isolated, niche sport to a multi-billion-dollar industry with a spot in the Olympics – both blessed by and burdened with a sense of legitimacy.

On the mechanical front, the mountain bike injected a sense of innovation and creativity. Mountain-bike inventors showed a remarkable willingness to appropriate

(continued on page 174)

Dusty trails are
*one of the hazards of
mountain-bike racing.*

The History of Head Protection

When hard surfaces began to replace the soft roads of the 19th century, head protection became a necessity. The first helmets were made of pith – a crushable Styrofoam-like material; not exactly ideal, but it softened the blow. Later, racing cyclists donned head coverings made from strips of leather-covered padding. They were hardly protective and rotted from sweat and rain. So, most riders – including professional racers – continued to go bare-headed, despite the risk.

Remarkably, it wasn't until the 1970s that manufacturers began to take the issue of bike helmet development seriously. The Snell Foundation in America issued the first bicycle helmet standard in 1970; but ironically only a non-vented, 2-pound (900 g) motorcycle helmet could pass the test. Few, if any, helmets therefore were certified to the new standard, and they were not available in bike shops.

Finally, in 1975, the Bell Biker, the first bicycling-specific, hard-shelled, crushable-foam-lined helmet, was released – and passed safety standards. Other manufacturers followed Bell's lead and through the years have made advances on the form. The hard outer shell has become lighter, more vents have been added and adjustable fastening systems now lock helmets securely on the rider's head. Today's helmets are safe, stylish and comfortable.

Still, many professional cyclists persistently eschew helmet use, even in the light of high-profile tragic deaths such as that of Italian Fabio Casartelli in 1995 – preferring headbands, caps or the wind through their hair. That changed in 2003, however, when the UCI ruled that professional cyclists must wear hard-shell helmets in every race or face a fine.

For the general public, government legislation over cycling helmets can be controversial. Australia was the first country in the world to make the wearing of helmets mandatory in 1990; statistics show that while deaths and injuries fell as a result, so also did the popularity of cycling. In the UK, about 1 in 5 cyclists currently wears a helmet – the government takes the view that to make them compulsory would reduce the number of people choosing to cycle, with a corresponding drop in the health benefits that it brings as an activity.

Helmets have always *been mandatory for professional mountain-bike riders.*

innovations from a variety of walks of life and from history. Nearly every basic suspension configuration in the first 20 years of the sport owed something to the old yellowing diagrams and texts from the late 19th and early 20th century.

Designs and materials were liberally borrowed from the motorcycle world (disc brakes), sailing (carbon-fibre construction and monocoques) and the military (exotic materials such as titanium and magnesium). Since gaining legitimacy and popularity in the early 1990s, major new suspension designs have come at the rate of roughly one per year and show few signs of slowing.

Technology is also more rapidly being disseminated throughout the industry; disc brakes, virtually unavailable on any bike at any price 10 years ago, are now widespread. The spirit of exploration and innovation that mountain bikes brought to the sport has continued to drive the technological advancement of the machine to the point that the top-level racing bikes of today share much of their inspiration and execution with Formula One cars. Even the everyday bike found in bike shops shares many of the benefits of that technology. Bicycles today are lighter, more reliable and more fun to ride than ever before.

(left) Mountain-bike suspension *designs continue to evolve. This bike from Cannondale has two shocks.*

(right) The benefits of suspension *technology can best be felt on challenging, rocky trails like these.*

CHAPTER 4

THE ART
OF THE
CYCLE

By Nicholas Oddy

THE MACHINE

The relationship between art and the cycle is complex. There are many examples of fine art that use cycles as all or part of their subject matter, including a rich variety of commercial art that advertises and promotes cycling, as well as illustrative art produced for magazines and books.

Furthermore, cycles have inspired decorative arts and products, while for many enthusiasts and design pundits, cycles themselves count as art objects. Of course, it all depends on what your definition of *art* is. The cycle builder's art is very different from the fine art produced by Marcel Duchamp and Pablo Picasso, both of whom incorporated references to cycles in their work.

The bicycle: *one of the most affordable works of art in the world.*

The machine aesthetic *takes art out of the studio.*

The cycle, particularly the bicycle, has appealed to many design critics as an example of a 'machine aesthetic' in which beauty is the natural outcome of an uncompromised and undecorated mechanical form. In fact, the cycle, like all man-made objects, is subject to human tastes and fashions, but its *seeming* simplicity disguises this. Those who think of the machine itself as a work of art usually think in the traditional manner that art means skill as well as beauty. They tend not only to look at the machine as a whole but also to derive much satisfaction from details that point to the skill of the maker and the quality of material, such as the lugwork, expert welding, crisply formed components and little idiosyncratic touches that separate the first division from the rest.

Extra pleasure may be derived from the knowledge and experience that separates the connoisseur from the novice or the philistine who may assume that all bicycles are much the same.

Frame-builders transform *metal with precision to create machine artwork.*

THE BUILDERS AND THEIR WARES

The modern cycle has its roots in the 1817 bicycle design of German Count Karl von Drais. Von Drais's 'running machine' had some attention paid to its looks, even in its earliest form – von Drais recommended that machines be painted in patriotic national colours. However, credit should probably go to Londoner Denis Johnson for giving careful consideration to both the practicality and beauty of the machine, which has become a hallmark of the cycle builder ever since. Johnson's machines, known as 'hobby-horses', enjoyed a brief but significant vogue in 1819. They used more metal components than von Drais's and were carefully shaped in sweeping curves, which allowed the machines to take on a lighter and more elegant appearance while also looking quick.

The frame-builder's ability to make the machine look light and fast, even when stationary, is essential to the art of cycle design. Johnson's machines and their riders also inspired and encouraged much interest from illustrators.

Two periods of cycle production stand out as providing the most aesthetically pleasing and satisfying examples of the art – these were on either side of the high-wheeled machine created in the 1870s and early 1880s. Both were notable in that the machines of those times were notoriously unsatisfying to ride, particularly the one that came later, but were hard to beat for sheer elegance and proportion. This raises the spectre of taste. Many believe the high-wheeler itself is in a class of its own, while many others consider the European lightweight cycle of the 1950s to be the

With its simple lines, *the 'running machine', also known as a 'Draisienne', was as much craft as early 19th-century technology.*

London gentlemen exercising *at 'Johnson's Pedestrian Hobby-Horse Riding School' (1819).*

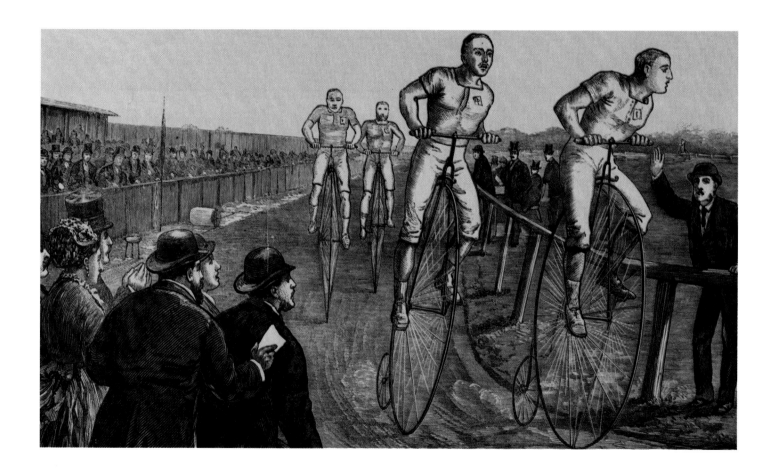

pinnacle of beauty. For some, today's state-of-the-art track machines rise to the top. All have their merits, but I suppose that I like the velocipede of the mid 1860s and the hard-tyred safety of the late 1880s because of their aesthetic triumphs over their deficiencies.

Both types of machine were very heavy and unresponsive to ride. While this is excusable in the case of the velocipede, which was made at a time when it was the only design available, it is less so in the case of the hard-tyred safety, which was produced simultaneously with the high-wheeler. Comparing the three, the high-wheeler is

a design form that, because of the fineness of the driving wheel and its dominance over the rest of the machine, it is difficult to get wrong. (Even a dog of a high-wheeler looks good at a few paces.) High-wheelers are differentiated only by their craftsmanship and minor details. Whereas most all-metal machines were plain black, the wooden-wheeled velocipede was more subject to the aesthetic manipulation of its components, which tended toward the carriage-building practices of bright paint and bold lining.

But for sheer variation, where the best is truly magnificent and the worst truly

execrable, the hard-tyred safety, in both bicycle and tricycle form, is a study in what makes a beautiful machine. The combination of hard tyres and clumsy chains of the early safeties did their riders no favours. However, the safeties could be geared up to go faster than a high-wheeler, even if a disproportionate amount of energy was used in doing so. Most riders were attracted by this potential speed, while a growing number of new riders were attracted by the lack of distance to the ground. To illustrate how important the look of the safety was to its market, we need only consider the

High-wheelers *were aesthetic triumphs, despite their practical difficulties. Here, early racers make their way rather precariously round a racecourse.*

pioneering designs of Englishman Harry John Lawson in the 1870s (the Lawson Bicyclette), which were dismissed for their ungainly appearance rather than their technical potential. It required the marketing skills of John Kemp Starley (nephew of James Starley, see page 150) to sell the concept of the chain-driven safety as a potentially faster machine than the high-wheeler with his Rover bicycle. Once this had been accepted, designs for chain-driven safeties proliferated. The combination of thin tubing and large diameter slender rims with narrow hard tyres is particularly pleasing.

Possibly because of the rough ride that one could expect from a low machine with no suspension, manufacturers were keen to experiment with curved tubes and long, sweeping handlebars that looked elegant and racy and absorbed vibration. Manipulating the components to look good rather than to perform any better became a particular art.

French arms manufacturer *Manufrance created this curvaceous beauty, the Hirondelle. 'L'Hirondelle' is the French word for the swallow, and it is easy to see the similarities between bird and bicycle.*

DA VINCI'S SKETCH
More Mystery than the Mona Lisa

Renaissance man Leonardo da Vinci is remembered as an artistic genius whose strokes of brilliance include the *Mona Lisa* and *The Last Supper*. This tends to overshadow the fact that this accomplished artist was also one of the greatest scientific minds of all time. In an era when the only choice for transportation was to go by foot or by pack animal, da Vinci created sketches of an aeroplane, a helicopter, a parachute and, some believe, a bicycle.

Though father-and-son Parisian carriage makers Pierre and Ernest Michaux are typically credited with developing the modern bicycle in the 1860s, a rough draft of a chain-driven, pedal-powered, two-wheeled machine was found in 1966 among da Vinci's writings for the government. Historians date the sketch back to the 1490s – about 370 years before the first velocipede rolled out.

Today, questions abound as to whether the bike drawing is da Vinci's brainchild, a student's creation, or an enormous hoax. The line drawing was discovered among other cartoon-like doodles filling the margin of da Vinci's *Codex Atlanticus*, a collection of sketches of weapons, aspects of warfare and

other devices. The name 'Salai', one of Leonardo's prized pupils, was penned on the back of the page. Some historians speculate that Salai had just copied the two-wheeled wonder from one of his master's many now-lost designs. Sceptics, however, argue the drawing is nothing but a fake – a modern-day hoax designed to further elevate popular perception of da Vinci's genius.

Since most of his work went unpublished, the world will likely never unravel the mystery of da Vinci's sketch. But based on the vast collection of inventive scientific musings he left behind, one thing is clear: a bicycle was certainly not beyond the realm of his imagination.

Did da Vinci *or one of his students sketch the first two-wheeler?*

187

A significant development of the hard-tyred period was the introduction of open-framed ladies' machines. These lent themselves to elegant and curvy forms, as is particularly well-illustrated by the French Hirondelle bicycle (pictured page 186). Best of all in this period were the tricycles by the great manufacturers such as Singer in the UK. Magnificent in proportion, detail and layout, they were wonderful objects to look at but hell to ride any distance!

Open-framed machines continued to challenge the cycle builder, given that they were inherently weak and given to 'whip'. Attempts to correct this have often produced artful results, not least of which is the so-called *mixte* lightweight frame of the 1930s, which is still made today. Even the classic semi-curved, or 'loop', format, typical of ladies' roadsters from 1890–1950 and still common in the Netherlands, makes a cheaply made machine into a worthwhile object.

Hard-tyred safeties were state-of-the-art adult machines for their time, but for the art of dressing up a machine, the peculiarly American phenomenon of the balloon-tyred bicycle was unrivalled. This bicycle was aimed

An incredible example *of streamlining, the Schwinn Aerocycle was created for the 1933–34 World's Fair held in Chicago, USA.*

at young people aspiring to travel quickly. The American motorcycle-style bicycle had been developing for two decades before the Schwinn Aerocycle (pictured page 189) was launched in 1933. Typical of other heavily styled goods produced during the Great Depression, it was probably more than a coincidence that the concept of stylistic obsolescence was considered a tool for economic recovery. The success of the Schwinn inspired others to follow suit for a generation. Like the hard-tyred safety, the results are impressive. Today, balloon-tyred bikes are collected as decorative art object.

Cycle connoisseurs who value efficiency are often drawn to the European lightweight cycle; the classic period of its production exactly parallels that of the balloon-tyred bike. Even though they are often more than half a century old, these machines, built on

While not necessarily expensive, *bicycles such as these in Amsterdam have a timeless elegance.*

slender racing rims with multiple-speed derailleur gears and dropped racing bars, still look quite modern. Although some were built in large factories, most were the products of small frame-building workshops, often under the control of a builder-owner whose surname became that of the machine. This more closely aligns the lightweight-bicycle collector with the fine art collector, in that the machines are products of named individuals. Experts can spot a particular builder's technique, or 'hand', in a frame the same way that decorative and fine art connoisseurs can in artwork. This lightweight 'tradition' continues to this day, as individual builders continue to produce custom-made frames in small numbers. The skill, workmanship and elegance of the resulting product continue to represent the best of the cycle builder's art.

DEPICTIONS OF CYCLING

When Denis Johnson presented his improved design of the Draisienne to the London market in 1819, it gained immediate attention not only from the fashionable young men who became associated with it (hence the nickname 'dandy horse'), but also from commentators more interested in its comic potential. The result was the production of a remarkable amount of hobby-horse-related artifacts and artwork.

Of these, the most significant by far are the prints made by publishers such as Thomas Tegg. Roger Street, in his seminal study of the hobby-horse, lists almost 100 prints – most of them satirical and most published in 1819. These prints were used to provide images for makers of trinkets and accessories, some of which remained popular well after the hobby-horse had gone out of fashion. Hobby-horse images appeared commonly on earthenware ceramics and small personal goods such as snuff and patch boxes like that pictured on the left.

Playing up *their comic potential, British publisher Thomas Tegg found a lucrative market for his studies of the hobby-horse and its practitioners.*

Cycling Memorabilia

As with many objects, from the rare and highly prized to the humble and everyday, the bicycle has its own incredibly colourful subculture of collectors. Bike collectors are no different from other types of collectors in that collecting is often a course that chooses them, rather than the other way around. 'I came across a bicycle that I liked but knew nothing about and I simply bought it. It went on from there and like most people I searched to find something that was like it or associated with it and ended up with a collection,' said Pryor Dodge, a New York-based musician and author who specializes in collecting bikes and artwork from the 19th century.

Satisfaction in collecting comes in many forms: for John Middleton it was a hobby shared with his wife that 'got out of hand', growing into what is now Britain's largest cycling museum, home to more than 400 different machines and thousands of pieces of cycling paraphernalia that the couple have collected over the years. Housed in an old Victorian railway station in Cornwall, the museum's collection ranges from the early to the modern. Curiosities like the tandem-tricycle (designed with Victorian etiquette in mind), and a replica Penti-cycle, a machine with four small wheels surrounding one large 'penny farthing' wheel, provide interesting focus points. The Penti-cycle was used briefly by postmen in the 1880s, although as its rider was supposed to alternate between four-wheel-drive and unicycling on the larger wheel, it proved a short-lived mode of transport. Needless to say, there is an interesting story behind every bicycle in the museum.

Most collectors tend to break down the object of their desire into a few common categories: extremely rare bikes from the turn of the century and before; pre-war bikes; balloon-tyre bikes such as the Schwinn Phantom, or vintage lightweight racing and touring bikes. The Sting-Ray and early European racing bikes are emerging as the favourites of a younger generation of collectors.

Bicycles and related ephemera *are becoming increasingly collectable.*

Decorative items
*such as this lamp were
popular at the end of
the 19th century.*

Throughout the 19th century, this pattern repeated with every cycling craze, but the amount of satirical material diminished in proportion to that which celebrated cycles and cycling. The fact that cycling was largely a pastime of the wealthy throughout the century doubtless encouraged many craftsmen to try to tap the purses of its devotees. It is not unusual to find quite elaborate porcelain figures, marble timepieces, gold and silver jewellery and so on, designed around a cycling theme. Such items were particularly prolific during the bicycle boom of the mid-1890s, by which time there was a substantial and rapidly increasing number of female cyclists. Yet curiously, most of this type of decorative design was quite conservative in style, favouring the Rococo and the Neo-Classical despite the modernity of its subject matter.

THE COMMERCIAL ARTISTS

High-quality, cycling-inspired decorative goods lasted longest in France and Germany where Art Nouveau, Secessionist and even early Art Deco-style work was produced. However, once the cycle was relegated to being a poor man's transport in Europe and a child's plaything in America during the inter-war years, high quality ended in all but trophy design. Typical products of the mid-to late 20th century were generally nostalgic and conservative in design and third rate in quality, being aimed at the low end of the gift and souvenir market.

If decorative design was cautious, the opposite was true of commercial art used to sell cycles to the 'boom' market of the 1890s. The cycle industry was truly on the cutting edge of the discipline, only equalled by theatre and concert advertising – way ahead of areas that were to excel in the 20th century such as railway and shipping lines. The cycle industry equated its products with high fashion and modernity and thus led the way in art catalogue and colour-litho poster design. American manufacturers arguably led the field using cutting-edge graphics, particularly in catalogue design. The major American manufacturers were aggressive in the international market and more conscious of the value of high-quality advertising than most others. Major marques such as Crescent, Waverley and Victor employed the most noted commercial artists of the time, such as Will Bradley. American catalogues and advertising done in Art Nouveau, French revue, Japanese and aesthetic styles were commonplace but were carried out with a panache that made them highly popular.

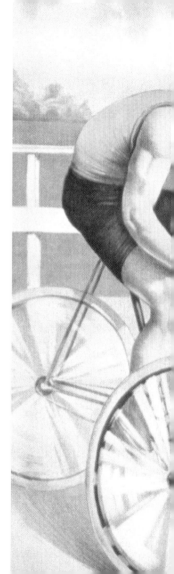

Early-20th-century *cycle advertising was as cutting edge as the most adventurous graphic design of the era.*

(left) **Naked or semi-naked** *female figures were not unusual in French cycling advertisements.*

(below) **This eye catching** *image associates the elegance and desirability of the female body with the bicycle.*

For sheer innovation and outrageous imagery, American cycle advertising paled in comparison to the French litho posters of the period – naked or almost naked female figures were not unusual; symbolism, often of a blatant and morally suspect kind, abounded. The famous poster for Gladiator Cycles (facing page) is probably the best known of these.

The links between the artistic avant-garde and bicycle production were fostered by manufacturers who commissioned bohemian fine artists to produce posters, the most famous being Henri de Toulouse-Lautrec for the French agency of the British Simpson Chain Syndicate.

Henri de Toulouse-Lautrec *produced some of the best-known bicycle related advertising such as this much-reproduced work for British Simpson Chain Syndicate.*

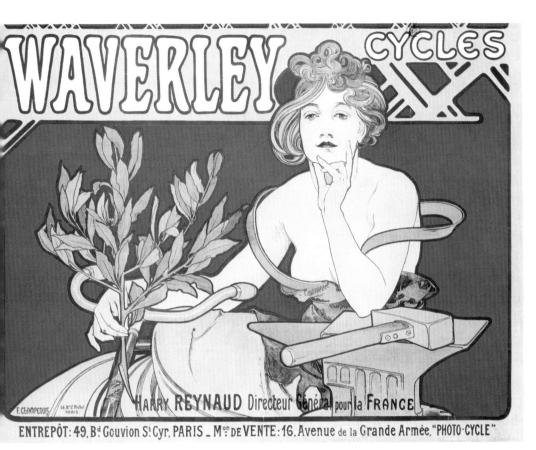

Indeed, it is worth noting that numerous non-French manufacturers other than Simpson commissioned special French posters through their French agencies; it is this practice that resulted in the well-known poster for Waverley by Czech Art Noveau artist Alphonse Mucha. Not surprisingly, the more dynamic French posters were not commonly seen outside of Paris and other French metropolitan centres. However, on an international level, critics saw them as significant, even at the time of their currency and they remain the most desirable cycle art to this day, appealing to a very broad audience and wealthy collectors.

Mucha's striking *Art Nouveau poster for Waverley is a high-benchmark for early cycle advertising.*

Our Common Thread

Although relatively few people ride bicycles every day, the two-wheeled companion leaves invisible tracks connecting nearly every man, woman and child. Almost everyone learns how to ride a bike and most people vividly remember their first two-wheeler. Part of our common bond, bicycles permeate our popular culture, and it's not difficult to pick out shiny triangular frames in our art, our entertainment and our literature.

Childhood books, in particular, are brimming with bicycles. Colourful, mischievous characters like Curious George, created more than 60 years ago by Hans and Margret Rey (who themselves fled Nazi Germany on bicycles), carry out their devilish deeds atop two wheels. Classic American storytellers like Mark Twain wrote entire essays on their bicycle follies. Author Enid Blyton's well-loved series of books The Famous Five and The Secret Seven, featured children who roamed all over the English countryside on their bicycles, solving mysteries as they went. Sometimes, even the bike alone was enough to be entertaining, as was the case with the notorious, never ridden but much talked about Klein mountain bike that hung in the apartment of Jerry Seinfeld, star of the US sitcom Seinfeld, for most of the show's nine-year run.

With their playful colours, shiny gears and simple architecture, bicycles have caught the eye of many an artist, as well. Perhaps the most famous and certainly the most simple, artistic rendition of a bicycle was the whimsical bike rider created by pop artist Keith Haring. His image of a person crouched down on two wheels is evocative of how devoted cyclists feel about their bikes – joyfully part of the machine.

As we advance into the 21st century, the bicycle rolls along with us as a quiet visual reminder of one thing we all have in common.

It's no coincidence *that the ever-mischievous Curious George is often seen riding a bicycle.*

THE ILLUSTRATORS

Less dramatic but equally skilled are the illustrations produced largely for the cycle press. Cycling was probably the first modern sport to develop a specialized press with a broad range of magazines and newspapers devoted wholly to it. During the 1880s, this became well established enough for some titles to commission regular illustrators whose line drawings have become the benchmark of cycling depiction. The English illustrator George Moore was probably the first to become a 'name', and in much the same style, the Anglo-American Joseph Pennell's work is well known through the books written by him and his wife, Elizabeth, on their various tricycling and bicycling adventures in the 1880s and 1890s. In the first half of the 20th century, Frank Patterson's drawings for the British weekly *Cycling* have come to evoke all the aspirations of cycling at the time. Much of his work survives today and is still affordable for those who want to own an original piece of art by one of the great names of cyclo-illustration. The art continues, but with the advances made in photography and colour printing, there is far less need for illustrators to produce work at the rate of their predecessors.

(left) Joseph Pennell *at work on a drawing in his studio.*

(right) One of Pennell's *works in which riders of high-wheelers parade before a lively crowd.*

FINE ART AND CYCLES

Probably the first time that cycles became a subject of fine art was during the period of the velocipedes in the second half of the 1860s.

A renowned image of the period was a painting of a well-known and wealthy French courtesan, Blanche d'Antigny, posed aside a Michaux-type machine wearing divided garments. The portrait was clearly intended to make a statement of d'Antigny's modernity, fashionability, independence and daring. Surprisingly though, painted portraits including bicycles were rare, even in the 1890s, when large numbers of wealthy women took to cycling. Perhaps unwilling to appear as bold as d'Antigny, few women chose to have themselves painted with their machines.

Two smart ladies *pose with their bikes in front of a wooded backdrop.*

Or perhaps it was because cycling portraiture was almost entirely the preserve of the new art of photography. The modernity of both was seen as complementary – photography as a new form of mechanical reproduction undermined the traditional form of the painted portrait and moreover the camera proved perfectly suited to capture objects in motion. Thus it is not surprising that many late-19th-century professional photo portraits of riders with their machines are still easily found.

(right) Invented and perfected *in parallel, the bicycle and the camera have had a stunning partnership.*

(left) A lady dressed *for riding her bicycle in this 1895 photograph.*

More typical of this period are paintings of generalized cycling scenes such as fashionable riders promenading in parks – for instance Jean Beraud's *Le Chalet du Cycle au Bois de Boulogne* (below). The Bois du Boulogne park in Paris is still popular with cyclists today.

Beyond his role as commercial artist for the British Simpson Chain Syndicate (see page 199), Henri de Toulouse-Lautrec produced a body of work depicting track cycling, its promoters and its participants. Quite apart from the important commercial considerations, Toulouse-Lautrec's interest was fired by the modernity, popularity and decadence of cycle racing, where doping was freely indulged and corruption was rife. Many events were seen as almost as morally bankrupt as Toulouse-Lautrec's other interest, revue bars.

Beraud pictures *cyclists in the Bois de Boulogne in Paris.*

LANCE ARMSTRONG
A Portrait of Motion

No book on cycling would be complete without Lance Armstrong. Armstrong has claimed his fifth Tour de France victory and many predict the champion from Texas will roll on to an unprecedented sixth. But his dominance in the hardest race on earth is merely a sidebar to his most amazing feat – a comeback from cancer.

Armstrong had all the makings of a rising star. The Golden Boy from America was a professional triathlete by age 16 and just six years later was a pro cyclist, holding 10 titles, including the US Pro Championship, World Champion (the youngest ever) and a stage victory at the Tour de France. He continued winning races and was named American Male Cyclist of the Year by *VeloNews* in 1995.

The next year his life would change forever. Forced from the bike by excruciating pain, Armstrong learned that he had advanced testicular cancer that had spread to his lungs and brain. His chances to live, let alone ride, were slim. But the tenacious Texan endured aggressive treatment including surgeries and intensive chemotherapy. Though physically depleted, his mental reserves swelled. The cancer went into remission and the raging competitor emerged.

Armstrong returned to the 1999 Tour de France and shocked the world with a no-holds-barred victory, followed by four more in the successive years.

Although his story is still being written, he will be an inspiration for the ages. Armstrong supports other cancer sufferers through the Lance Armstrong Foundation for research and education.

VITAL STATS

NATIONALITY: American

DATE OF BIRTH: 18 September 1971

CAREER VICTORY HIGHLIGHTS: Tour de France: 1999, 2000, 2001, 2002, 2003; Midi Libre: 2002; Dauphiné: 2002; Tour of Switzerland: 2001; Tour du Pont: 1995, 1996; World Road Champion: 1993

BICYCLE ART TODAY

Over the last century, the use of cycles in fine art has moved away from the straight depictions of the 1890s toward a more conceptual role. In the early 20th century, it was still enough of a dynamic machine to be the subject of Italian Futurism, a movement that celebrated the mechanization of society.

The linking of human energy, vulnerability and balance that the bicycle represents creates a powerful resonance of meaning that has been exploited by artists as diverse as Fernand Léger and Robert Rauschenberg. Significantly, it was one of the first objects to be employed by artists as a 'readymade'. Coined by Marcel Duchamp, the term indicates manufactured or found objects used in sculpture to play on the prosaic and commonplace nature of the object to force the viewer to reassess and question its meaning.

(left) Robert Rauschenberg's *Pop Art has often featured bicycles.*

(right) Fernand Léger *often depicted modern, urban, technological culture.*

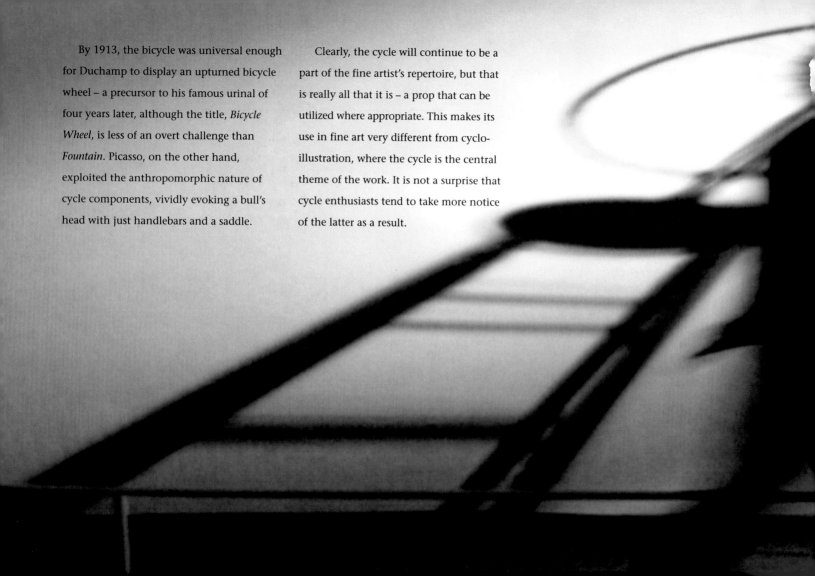

By 1913, the bicycle was universal enough for Duchamp to display an upturned bicycle wheel – a precursor to his famous urinal of four years later, although the title, *Bicycle Wheel*, is less of an overt challenge than *Fountain*. Picasso, on the other hand, exploited the anthropomorphic nature of cycle components, vividly evoking a bull's head with just handlebars and a saddle.

Clearly, the cycle will continue to be a part of the fine artist's repertoire, but that is really all that it is – a prop that can be utilized where appropriate. This makes its use in fine art very different from cyclo-illustration, where the cycle is the central theme of the work. It is not a surprise that cycle enthusiasts tend to take more notice of the latter as a result.

CHAPTER 5

MOUNTAIN BIKES

By Zapata Espinoza

WHEN IT ALL BEGAN

The story of mountain biking is full of events, places and personalities. Its history – decades old – was innocent, pure and without bias. By the mid-1970s, when it began anew, it was innocent no more.

The question of when mountain biking was born remains one of the great two-wheel mysteries. For all we know, it could have been in the middle of a Tour de France back in the 1920s when the first Italian to win the acclaimed race, Ottavia Bottecchia and his hard-man cohorts were pedalling along dirt roads up the Alps, suffering in a manner not unlike today's TransAlp mountain-bike racers.

Maybe it was on the outskirts of Paris in the 1950s when members of the Velo Cross Club Parisien mounted primitive suspension parts on their bikes and gathered for weekend forays on the scrambles courses after their motorcycling brethren had gone home for the day. These were the forbears of the mountain-cross racers we now watch on the sports channel.

The Velo Cross Club Parisien *may have been the first mountain-bike club.*
They definitely had the outsider spirit associated with fat-tyre pioneers.

The answer remains elusive – and we're better off because of it. One thing is clear: in the beginning, it was a simple matter of dirt roads and a need to get somewhere else, with no other way to get there but through the open countryside. If we dismiss the need for dates, we can more simply trace the roots of the sport in these terms: cycling off-road for work became fun and then technology evolved to make it fast and with purpose. That is really when the sport of mountain biking was born. Although the trails are important, they've always been there; focusing on them alone would be tantamount to conversing about goat herding. No! We're talking about mountain biking and to analyse the subject is to acknowledge the arrival of sport-specific technology. Gears, tyres, frame designs and, of course, suspension are the true markers of the sport's progress.

From the Velo Cross Club *to world champion John Tomac, the sport is all about adrenaline.*

FROM MARIN TO THE BUTTE

True, the San Francisco suburb of Marin County, USA, is widely credited as the birthplace of modern mountain biking. However, the original 'tilters' in Crested Butte, Colorado, probably still laugh at the thought. For while the Marin hippies were bolting derailleurs onto their 1940 Klunker bikes to have downhill races on Mt. Tamalpais, the Butte hippies were taking their bikes up and over the treacherous 12,700-foot (3,810-m) elevation of Pearl Pass and into Aspen.

As Crested Butte local Don Cook says, 'The Marin guys were experimenting with technology, but it wasn't until they got here that the technology was introduced to the kind of terrain that would define the sport.'

(continued on page 222)

Before *it was a haven for dot-com millionaires, Marin County, California, was home to mountain biking's pioneers.*

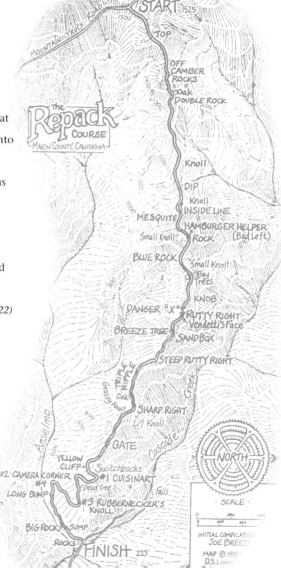

Centuries in the Making

Off-road enthusiasts typically credit Marin County, California, bike gurus Gary Fisher, Tom Ritchey and Joe Breeze as the 'fathers of mountain biking'. True, this ingenious trio developed the first bikes that were built, sold and marketed specifically for trail riding. But dirt-loving cyclists had been tooling together fat tyres and beefy bikes for at least 100 years before anyone knew those three names.

Some say Scottish veterinarian John B. Dunlop invented the first 'mountain bike' in 1887, when he fitted an inflatable piece of rubber hose over the solid tyres on his son's bicycle. The air cushion provided much-needed suspension for the rough roads and paths of the time. By the early 1950s, there was off-road racing in Paris, as the Velo Cross Club Parisien juiced up their bikes and tested their mettle on a course that was remarkably similar to a modern mountain-bike circuit. In Britain, the Rough Stuff Fellowship was formed in 1955. This was a group of cycling enthusiasts who wanted to get away from roads and cycle on tracks and byways. Still active today, the RSF publishes route guides and brings together groups from different parts of the country such as the Peak District 'Bogtrotters' or the Scottish 'Vagabonds'.

In America, the first mountain bike was probably developed by John Finley Scott in 1953. He added flat handlebars, balloon tyres and cantilever brakes to a Schwinn World diamond frame and christened it the 'Woodsie Bike'. He remained alone in his pursuit until the early '70s, when a band of dirt lovers, called the Cupertino Riders, cruised through Southern California on beefy race bikes built by Russ Mahon. That's where Fisher, Ritchey and Breeze got the idea and ran with it, starting a mountain-bike fever that would spread worldwide in the early 1980s, when bike manufacturers Specialized and Univega unveiled two Japanese-built bicycles for less than $1,000 (around £620). The rest, as they say, is history.

Pearl Pass *above Crested Butte, Colorado, is as popular a destination for mountain bikers as ever.*

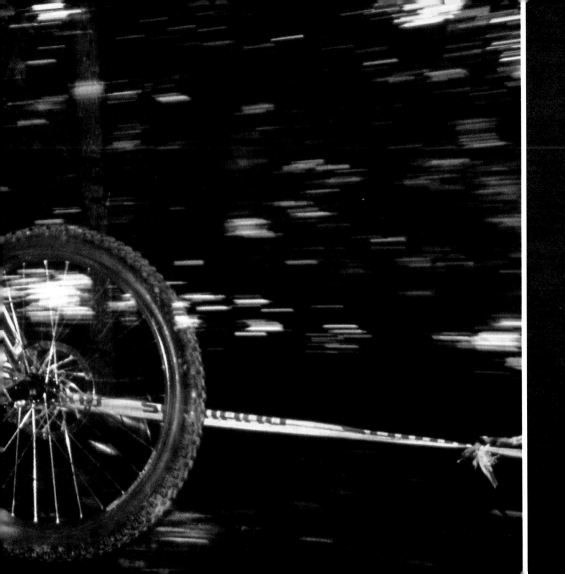

'The mountain bike
didn't just create
a new bicycle, it
humanized cycling.'

JOE BREEZE

Both experiences point to the moment when passionate off-road cyclists started tinkering with their bikes. The cycling world was about to enter a new phase that would forever alter its popularity. And when road-racing cyclist Joe Breeze welded together the first mountain-bike frame in 1977, its unique qualities set the frenzy for specific mountain-bike equipment in motion. There would be no turning back.

Luckily for us, the Marin mountain bikers were all road geeks before they tasted off-road pleasure. The likes of pioneers Gary Fisher, Charlie Kelly, Tom Ritchey and Breeze could never leave well enough alone. The bikes they rode seldom used the same setup from week to week due to their constant tinkering and parts swapping. By the end of the 1970s, all of Marin was abuzz with the off-road sensation. The news of the mountain-bike creation could no longer be confined to the small brigade that had nurtured it for the previous six years.

From Repack *through to the latest 24-hour race, founding father Gary Fisher still practises what he preaches.*

With access to trails *and remote places previously inaccessible, mountain biking took off in a big way.*

'Keeper of the Flame'
Don Cook is co-director of the Mountain Bike Hall of Fame in Crested Butte, Colorado.

ENTER THE ENTREPENEURS

The year was 1982. BANG! It had begun. Cycling entrepreneur Mike Sinyard took the mountain-bike frame he'd bought from road-racer and frame-builder Tom Ritchey and sent it to Japan to have some cheap copies made. Granted, motorcycle racer Mert Lawwill had made his Pro Cruiser five years earlier, while manufacturer Univega was playing with off-road bikes and the Schwinn bicycle company began marketing their Sidewinder mountain bike as early as 1981.

But Sinyard's 'Specialized Stumpjumper' was the bike that got the mass-production ball rolling. By the mid-80s every known bike maker had jumped on the mountain-bike bandwagon. Unfortunately, with no precedent to draw upon, very few of them had any idea exactly what they were doing.

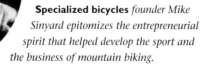

Specialized bicycles *founder Mike Sinyard epitomizes the entrepreneurial spirit that helped develop the sport and the business of mountain biking.*

Beginning in *1981, Specialized's Stumpjumper brought the mountain bike to the masses.*

Even as late as the early 1990s, many mountain bikes suffered from the effects of being designed by ageing road geeks who treated the mountain bike as a passing fad, a novelty. Little did they know!

However, the small bike makers who showed true passion for off-road cycling would themselves become the fledgling sport's biggest personalities. Frame-builders

More than *20 years later, the Stumpjumper retains the name but not much else from the original model.*

like Chris Chance, Charlie Cunningham,
Doug Bradbury, Richard Cunningham, Keith
Bontrager and, of course, Gary Fisher and
Tom Ritchey, helped fuel the sport's soon-
to-be explosive growth with wonderfully
designed, sport-specific bikes. These were
some of the key players who planted the
early seeds of what would become a multi-
million-dollar cottage industry.

The small independents *who put the
soul into mountain biking:* (clockwise
from top far-right) *Keith Bontrager, Chris
Chance, Charlie Cunningham, Richard
Cunningham and Doug Bradbury.*

SUSPENSION

In 1989, seven years after the Stumpjumper's arrival at the Long Beach bike show, a radical, previously unimagined new bike was wheeled into the same convention hall – and the sport would never be the same.

While most manufacturers were still trying to work out what the ingredients were for even the most basic off-road bicycle, the guys from Kestrel rolled their fully suspended, carbon-fibre Nitro into their booth. Jaws dropped, heads shook and cameras clicked. It wasn't supposed to happen, at least not this soon.

Mountain bikes *with full suspension are a familiar sight today.*

Although the bike as a whole took top honours for the most innovative bike at the show, it was the RockShox suspension fork mounted on the front that would prove to have the most enduring impact. RockShox: no one would ever guess that what began in a cramped, dirty Santa Cruz garage would some day become a multinational company traded on the New York Stock Exchange. *(continued on page 232)*

Paul Turner *started his business to bring motorcycle-inspired front suspension to the mountain bike in his garage.*

JOHN TOMAC
A Wonder on Wheels

Imagine a high-speed champion runner racing off after his Olympic gold medal wins to compete and crush the field in a city marathon. That's the kind of bike rider John Tomac was – a legend who blasted through traditional boundaries between cycling niches and forever changed the face of mountain-bike racing.

Emerging from the BMX scene, where he won his first national title in 1984 at the age of 16, 'Johnny T' has topped the podium at more mountain-bike races than anyone in racing history. During a time when XC racers were health-conscious featherweights and downhillers were heavily muscled party boys, Tomac grabbed top honours in both disciplines, winning the national XC title in 1996 and the downhill title in 1997.

Early in his career, he even hopped aboard skinny tyres, splitting his time between professional road- and mountain-bike racing. Again, he was an instant success, capturing the Best Young Rider title at the Coors Classic Prologue (San Francisco) in 1988. US magazine *VeloNews* crowned him the world's top all-round rider that same year.

Ever the rugged and often eccentric, individualist, Tomac was willing to race equipment most image-conscious racers wouldn't be seen dead on. Some experiments, like drop road-racing bars on his mountain bike, never caught on. But others, most notably using a full suspension rig to crush his competitors at the downhill World Cup in 1993, changed racers' approach to speed and technology forever.

VITAL STATS

NATIONALITY: American

DATE OF BIRTH: 3 November 1967

CAREER VICTORY HIGHLIGHTS: US Road Championships: 1988; World Mountain-Bike Championships: 1988, 1990; US Cross-Country Championships: 1996; US Downhill Championships: 1997; US BMX Cruiser Championship: 1984

The impact of suspension on the bicycle industry in the late 1980s would, as a whole, be bigger than that of any other single product. It was the suspension element that also opened the floodgates for the throttle twisters to come rushing in.

Virtually every motorbike fan came to mountain biking with a shared experience: they'd ridden a bicycle off-road and found it to be not only uncomfortable, but unsafe as well. They knew there had to be a better way and with their wealth of knowledge and first-hand experience in the dynamics of riding two wheels over rough ground it was the motorcyclists who trumped the more traditionally minded bike riders on the sport's biggest advancement.

If left to the bike geeks themselves, suspension probably would never have happened, as the general feeling was that suspension added little more than a comfort factor that could not contribute to the efficiency of cycling. It was one thing for downhillers to use suspension, the pedal set thought, but really, was it called for anywhere else? The motorcycle guys, however, proved more than able to dispel that half-baked notion.

(left) Even the most *weight-conscious cross-country rider can appreciate the comfort and safety of a suspension fork.*

(right) Proud papa Gary Fisher *hoists two-time Olympic champion Paola Pezzo's full-suspension cross-country race bike.*

In 1993, when wily Frenchman Gilbert Duclos-Lassalle outsprinted Italian Franco Ballerini to win the infamous Paris–Roubaix road race on his LeMond road bike that was outfitted with special RockShox suspension forks, it looked as though mountain bike suspension would even conquer the tradition-bound world of European road racing. However, after a few years of wild experimentation (where a number of front- and full-suspension designs were tried), road-bike suspension faded into the background. Since Duclos-Lassalle's '93 victory, there have been no major wins on road bicycles outfitted with suspension. Due to the emphasis on minimal weight and maximum efficiency,

it's unlikely that suspension will become the norm for road racing anytime soon

By the year 2000, it was all about suspension. The sport of downhilling had morphed into something called *freeriding* and even elite cross-country (XC) riders were relying more and more on the performance benefits found with new, niche-specific suspension technology. Where the big air huckers were using coil-sprung, wet-bath suspension parts to get up to 10 inches (25 cms) of super plush front and rear travel, the XC-set were coming to terms with shorter travel air shocks with remote lockout and intricate valving providing a stable pedalling platform that was unprecedented.

(continued on page 238)

Frenchman Duclos-Lassalle *riding to victory in the 1993 Paris–Roubaix.*

Traditionally minded
*road racers such as
American George
Hincapie are reluctant
to use suspension
for even the most
difficult races.*

The Mountain Bike Moves On

In 1977, a British cycling journalist named Richard Grant went to California and returned with one of the early Marin County modified Schwinns. This may well have been the first mountain bike in Britain. Fellow bicycle enthusiast, author and magazine publisher Richard Ballantyne was also interested in the Californian bikes. In 1982, he imported one of Mike Sinyard's Specialized Stumpjumpers from the States. Through his extensive network of cycling contacts his enthusiasm for the new bike spread. He recommended the Stumpjumper to the two long-distance riders, Tim Gartside and Peter Murphy, who in 1982–83 completed an unsupported bike journey across the Sahara Desert using the new mountain bikes. Ballantyne continued to promote the fledgling sport, organizing the first mountain-bike race series in Britain, the Fat Tyre Five, in 1983. Today mountain bikers are a familiar sight across the UK, with the challenging terrain of regions like Wales and Scotland acting as a magnet for the sport's enthusiasts. Similarly, in Australia, the sport has been enthusiastically adopted by cyclists keen to interact with the stunning natural scenery and demanding outback trails.

But for the most ambitious amateur mountain-bikers, more of a challenge was needed, and so 24-hour races evolved, adding darkness and sleep deprivation to the difficulties of the trails. The concept was introduced in America with the '24 Hours of Canaan' held in West Virginia in 1992. It was an immediate success. Ex-sports masseur Patrick Adams saw one of the early races in the US, and brought the concept back to the UK. The 'Mountain Mayhem' race that he held in 1998 has grown into the biggest 24-hour race in Europe, attracting 1,800 riders in 2003. 'It's not just an event for riders, but a personal achievement,' Adams comments. He is keen to develop a global 24-hr championship series. For novices, the races are a rite of passage. And for everyone who loves the sport, they're just a roaring good time.

Part Le Mans, part Woodstock, *a 24-hour race is for anyone with a bike and a little Evel Knievel inside.*

OH, AND THE OUTDOORS

More important than technology, it is the places to ride that make the whole endeavour worthwhile.

From the rolling hills of England and Wales to the rugged mountains of Scotland, from the northern-European flatlands to the dizzying alpine peaks, the ride is the take-home benefit most worth savouring. Whether you're catching air in Morzine in the French Alps, splashing through a creek in Australia, or losing some skin on a mountain trail in New Zealand, riding your bike off-road is what makes the mountain-bike experience complete. Virtually none of the breakthroughs in frame or suspension technology would mean a thing if there weren't so many fabulous places to put them to use. Far and away, the inherent challenge of the trails is the experience that we live for – a challenge that far outshines the greatness of anything designed on a computer or marketed in a conference room. Long before full-suspension bikes with lightweight carbon-fibre frames and brakes ever showed up at the Slickrock Trail in Moab, the trails were already providing the more intrepid with a wonderful wilderness experience.

The natural landscape *accessible to the mountain biker can be awe-inspiring.*

TO THE RESCUE

Unfortunately, the very essence of the sport is also the very thing that nearly doomed it. It didn't take long for enthusiastic mountain bikers to come into conflict with other, more traditional user groups out on the trails. Run-ins with hikers, equestrians and conservationists would soon become the most serious threat to the sport's growth and popularity both in the US and in other countries around the world.

Luckily, networks of trail advocates, not unlike the cottage industry of designers and manufacturers who were responsible for so much of the sport's technological growth, came to the forefront of the land-access battle, which loomed large and threatening in the off-road world.

With trail use *at an all-time high, conflicts between user groups continue to escalate.*

Unfortunately, trail advocacy as an activity is far less inspiring than the riding itself. But for the sport to survive, it had to be done and thankfully, individuals such as Don Douglass and Gibson Anderson, the two men credited with forming the International Mountain Bicycling Association (IMBA) in 1988, took an early lead in the effort. The IMBA's philosophy is to bring out the best in mountain biking by encouraging low-impact riding, volunteer trail participation, cooperation among different trail users and innovative trail management solutions. Based in Colorado, USA, the IMBA's worldwide network includes 32,000 individual members, over 450 bicycle clubs and more than 100 corporate partners. Working in partnership with other organizations like the UCI, or Mountain Bike Australia, for example, the IMBA provides a unified sense of purpose, guidelines for sensible trail use, and a certain amount of political muscle to ensure that trails stay open and are used responsibly.

Specialized was one of only a handful of bike companies who shared this vision before the movement went mainstream. Their 'Peace on Dirt' campaign provided just the sort of positive PR that mountain-biking needed to take an early foothold in the land-access crisis.

Don Douglass   **Alan Armstrong**

Alan Armstrong *was inducted into the Mountain Bike Hall of Fame in 1993 for his efforts to protect the trails in the San Gabriel Mountains near his home in Pasadena, California.*

Freeriders *like these often catch the worst criticism from user groups that oppose mountain biking.*

'We were a tribe,

young and ecstatic,

and at that moment,

the world was ours.'

ZAPATA ESPINOZA
Mountain Bike magazine, December 2001

INMATES IN CHARGE: HOW THE INDUSTRY EVOLVED

The year was 1990 and in a quiet corner of southwest Colorado, the town of Durango held the first ever International Cycling Union (UCI)-sanctioned world mountain-bike championships. The rainbow jersey, coveted by road racers for decades, would now be awarded to both cross-country and downhill dirt bikers. We had arrived!

The Mountain Bike Hall of Fame,
a long-range goal for any top racer.

A watershed in the sport's cultural history, not unlike when suspension was introduced, Durango not only marked the birth of the sport on a global basis, but it also heralded the arrival of the racer and bike company as household names.

Organized races had been held for the previous decade, but it wasn't until Durango that athletes and specific products attained cult status. Riders like Ned Overend, Greg Herbold and Juli Furtado, and manufacturers such as Yeti Cycles, Manitou and Onza were now icons of a sport soon to burst from its mountain origins.

(left) One of the top *professionals to make Durango, Colorado, his home, Myles Rockwell was downhill world champion in 2000.*

(right) By the age *of 26, French rider Anne-Caroline Chausson had won a dozen downhill and slalom world championships.*

An Overnight Sensation

Juli Furtado's motto was 'The slower you go, the more likely it is you'll crash.' One of mountain biking's most ferocious competitors, Furtado bolted from obscurity to dominance in a sport she claimed to have tried just because the 'guys were cute'.

In reality it was problems with her knees that drove her to the bike. After earning a spot on the 1982 US Ski Team at just 15, she pushed too hard and blew out both hinges, leading to a forced retirement at 21. As the saying goes, if you can't walk, you can bike; so Furtado muscled her way into road cycling and became an instant success – snatching the US National Championship in 1989. The following year she returned to the ski resorts, only this time on a mountain bike.

Furtado was an unstoppable force on the mountain-bike circuit – crushing the field in her first year as a pro, winning the 1990 US Cross-Country Championships. Three years later, she made cycling history capturing the top podium spot in 17 consecutive American and international races. She was a five-time national champion; three-time World Cup champ and even won the World Downhill Championships one year. In 1996, she realized her dream of making the Olympics in mountain biking's debut year.

Sadly, Furtado's remarkable run ended almost as abruptly as it began. In late 1997, after a season plagued by fatigue, ill health and misdiagnosis, Furtado learned she had systemic lupus, an auto-immune disease that causes pain and inflammation. Her racing career was over. Today, Furtado lives on in the sport through her own line of women-specific mountain bikes.

VITAL STATS

NATIONALITY: American

DATE OF BIRTH: 14 April 1967

CAREER VICTORY HIGHLIGHTS: World Downhill Championships: 1992; US National Championships: 1991, 1992, 1993, 1994, 1995; World Cross-Country Championships: 1990; US National Road Championships: 1989

When the world championships visited
Italy the following year, race results spoke as
much about an athlete's personal abilities as
about the equipment they used. The battle
for territory in the mountain-bike market was
raging at full force and everyone wanted in.
Who would ever have envisioned road-racing
marques like Colnago and Campagnolo on
the winners' podium for a mountain-bike
race? It would only get crazier.

By the mid-90s, the mountain-bike
industry found itself on a fully-fledged rocket
propelled into the stratosphere. Mountain-
bike-specific magazines had evolved on every
continent. A Hall of Fame was established
in 1988 in Crested Butte, Colorado, USA.
And in 1996, cross-country mountain biking
skipped the demonstration status of most
young sports and qualified for a permanent
place in the Olympics.

Miguel Martinez
*hoists his bike
in delight, having
won the cross-country
race at the 2000
Sydney games.*

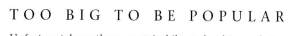

TOO BIG TO BE POPULAR

Unfortunately, as the mountain-bike rocketship made its turn into the late '90s, the fuel provided by events such as the Olympic inclusion would prove more flammable than energizing.

We'd grown so large, so quickly, that we seemed to have forgotten who we were, what we were doing and why we were doing it. Following the 1996 Olympics, the big business fracas – battles over athlete endorsements and the 'best bike' – that had enveloped the mountain-bike industry started to take its toll. All the mighty corporations that had invaded the sport when companies were showing big profits and going public were now – when they weren't getting kicked out – scrambling to get out. Corporate credentials were suddenly deeply unfashionable.

Corporate sponsorship *was key to the existence of high-level racing, but had the sponsorship become what racing was all about?*

In the haste to go big, people had forgotten that the sport's earliest success was brought about by a bunch of passionate bike freaks. The suits-and-ties that came in later were, for the most part, not in it for the right reasons. True, some of them may have learned to ride with clipless pedals, but they weren't close to the sport. They couldn't understand the value of bagging peaks in Crested Butte or that the experience was far more valuable than a hefty stock option. They'd retreat from the races at mid-day for cocktails or a game of golf while Mert Lawwill and Steve 'Gravy' Gravenites would be hanging out in the pits late into the night trying to improve the product.

By the late 1990s, at least a quarter of the companies that came along for the ride were suddenly gone. While each loss had its own reasons, it was apparent to the casual observer that too many companies were run either by businessmen who cared little for the sport itself, or by a bunch of cycling zealots who, while qualified as enthusiasts, proved less so as entrepreneurs. The simplest equation was that too many of the small guys had staked a claim based more on their technical know-how and ingenuity than on sound business skills.

Even though there was a large number of small businesses who went under, they could perhaps find some solace in the fact that in the decade that saw the sport's biggest growth, big-time companies like GT and Schwinn also somehow found themselves bankrupt – Schwinn twice!

In the end, it became obvious that more than just youthful enthusiasm and a sheer love of the sport were needed to sustain the business side of things.

The joy of winning *for this competitor is an important reminder of what the sport is really all about.*

Rolling along the Riviera

The official mountain-bike season typically wraps up by the end of summer, with many pros hanging up their wheels for the month of October before launching into off-season training. Some, however, make sure they have juice left in the tank for one of the biggest mountain-bike race festivals in Europe – the Roc d'Azur, a French classic that attracts the sport's most elite riders, as well as 10,000 other participants and more than 100,000 spectators to the Fréjus beach station along the French Riviera.

Created more than 15 years ago, the Roc d'Azur is held over a four-day period in mid-October each year. At the heart of it is the Roc d'Azur race, a 34-mile (55-km) loop renowned for its breathtaking beauty as well as for its harsh technical terrain. The course sweeps through the forest on singletrack and sends racers along the border of the

Mediterranean Sea, including a rough, traditional passage on the beach where throngs of spectators spend the day cheering. Along with the elite race, the Roc d'Azur offers something for riders of all ages and abilities. For those who prefer to take the trails at their own pace, there's the Rando

Roc, an untimed ramble to the cross-country race closing ceremony. Amateur riders can tackle a shorter 21-mile (35-km) course. And there's even a kids' mini race.

Along with the racing, riders and fans can check out BMX exhibitions, special events such as dances and the largest French trade fair for cyclists. The event has become so popular that it has become a tourist destination, with cycling enthusiasts booking holidays that include regional tours, meals, training rides and, of course, the race itself. Cyclists also are free to come ride the Roc d'Azur all season, though most would agree it's more fun when a few thousand enthusiasts are along for the ride.

The Roc d'Azur *sees as many as 10,000 riders sprint up the beach and rip through the mountains.*

THE NEW SAVIOUR –
SAME AS THE OLD SAVIOUR

In 1991, when *Mountain Bike* magazine was counting down the 15 most significant people in the sport, we didn't give the nod to some elite racer, rocket scientist, or corporate bigwig, but instead, to an old coot by the name of Victor Vincente of America (VVofA).

Having never heard of him, many people in the industry expressed shock over our choice. With all that the mountain-bike industry had accomplished over the years, how was it, they wondered, that we could laud someone with virtually no commercial or even social ties to the inside realm?

Precisely. VVofA, without a doubt, remains emblematic of the sport's roots that we felt it necessary to get back to. Though the paradigm of mountain biking had shifted an untold number of times in the previous decade, it seems to be honing in on a semblance of what many thought it was originally.

'Vincente is No. 1 in our book because from the beginning he's pursued poetry, not patents... He's gentle and freakish and wears his iconoclasm proud – which is the way a mountain-biking forefather should go.'

MOUNTAIN BIKE MAGAZINE
January 2001

While it's doubtful that many people enjoying the current mood swing were actually around 'back in the day', the shift is telling in terms of what they want their mountain-bike experience to be. Probably the most significant boost to the 'back to the roots' movement was the ascendancy of the 24-hour racing scene that brought a sense of camaraderie and carefree attitude that many felt had been lost over the years.

For sure, technological advances continue at a rapid pace, but following all the technology battles, the buyouts and the infighting, it seems that the sport of mountain biking has finally calmed down long enough to look in the mirror and see its true reflection – passion about having fun. And appreciating the natural world. Curiously, one of the sport's best attributes – its sense of smallness and community – seems to have worked against it because too often the sport was defined by the industry. Many enthusiasts felt trapped by the commercial side of things, which never had anything to do with enjoying a fantastic view from the mountain trails in Moab. Whatever deals were made at the trade show in Taiwan had no bearing on the ability of a person to go out and enjoy a ride in the great outdoors.

They might have *numbers on their chests, but the simple joy of being out there makes mountain biking the greatest way to spend a day.*

More recently, the sport seems to be back on track. Though the industry is still bent over, catching its breath from the last decade, it does so with an eye towards the future and hopefully, an eye towards doing things differently. While traditional racing continues at its roller-coaster pace, the new style of adventure and extreme races is taking hold.

What hasn't changed is the lure that has always made mountain biking so attractive in the first place. The primal impulse is felt by everyone who craves being outdoors. They're looking for adventure and the opportunity to get outside and have fun with their friends and family. The mountain bike remains the perfect vehicle for such pursuits because the mountains themselves provide the perfect reason to start pedalling.

One of the world's *finest mountain-bike rides, the Slickrock Trail, near Moab, Utah, USA.*

CHAPTER 6

THE
GREATEST
RACE

By James Startt

THE EARLY TOURS

A simple business lunch was all it took for two men to conceive of what would become the world's greatest bike race, or at least that's what history shows. In an old Paris brasserie called the Zimmer, Georges Lefèvre and Henri Desgrange concocted the idea of a 'Tour de France Cycliste'. The year was 1902.

Modelled after a Six-Day track race, Tour de France cyclists would leave the confines of a velodrome and loop around the entire country of France. In 1903, the first Tour – a 1,509-mile (2,428-km) affair split into six stages – seemed far-fetched at best, little more than a marketing coup for Lefèvre and Desgrange's newspaper *L'Auto*. But now, a century later, this unique bike race has become embedded in France's heritage and, according to official terminology, is considered the world's greatest annual sporting event.

Henri Desgrange

The first *Tour de France in 1903 was somewhat more informal than today's race.*

Cycling a century ago was, at best, a fledgling sport, centred primarily on the bicycle's efficiency as a mode of transportation. Races were largely confined to specially constructed velodromes. But at the end of the 19th century, the idea of racing on roads was growing. Participation also grew, attracting unexpected fans and competitors.

The late-19th-century painter Henri de Toulouse-Lautrec was an avid fan while Fauvist painter Maurice de Vlaminck reportedly rode the mythic Paris–Roubaix race. Cycling reviews in magazines such as *Velo* and *L'Auto* achieved average sales of around 25,000 – a healthy circulation rate even by today's standards. Each new race tried to outdo previous ones. Paris–Rouen was outdone by Bordeaux–Paris, a 400-mile (643-km) night-and-day affair. And then there was the seemingly endless 845-mile (1,200-km) Paris–Brest–Paris, where cyclists ventured from the French capital to the northwestern coastal town in Brittany and back. The Tour de France idea, however, was unthinkable – at least until that day in 1902 when Lefèvre and Desgrange thought of it. But the idea quickly grew and when they officially announced the race in January of

(continued on page 270)

During its first century *the Tour de France has developed its own mythology. This poster depicts past champions.*

Although Toulouse-Lautrec *died two years before the inaugural Tour de France, he was able to observe other early road races, as shown by this sketch.*

The May Feast

Perhaps nowhere on the planet are people as passionate about cycling as in Italy – home of cycling greats such as the legendary Fausto Coppi and current star Mario Cipollini, known as *il re leone* ('the lion king'). Italian bike frames such as Pinarello and Calnago rival works of art while the rolling spectacle that brings it all together with 43 million passionate Italian cycling fans is the Giro d'Italia.

Once deemed the 'May Feast' by poetic cyclist Bruno Raschi, the Giro is a treat for the senses. Like the Tour de France, it is an annual three-week stage race that features flat sprinting stages, time trials and impossibly high, gruelling mountain passes. Although the course changes from year to year, it always promises challenge and opportunity for racers of all specialties and generally covers around 2,000 miles (3,220 km) before ending in Milan. The Italian tour also features pre-race hoopla including at least 1,000 vehicles representing the media, cycling teams, technical assistance and, of course, the parade of advertisers tossing sweets and trinkets to onlookers along the course. Unlike the Tour, the Giro is considered accessible to the everyday fan. The entourage is considerably smaller, allowing cycling enthusiasts to get an up-close and personal view of their favourite competitors. And it's not uncommon for top riders to be available for pictures and autographs.

Some consider the Giro d'Italia more exciting than the Tour de France in that the field is wide open. Although there are always a few pre-race favourites, almost any strong candidate can and often does, take the top podium spot. Combine the ever-exciting racing with fervent fans and bright spring weather with a backdrop of superb food and great wine and it's easy to understand how this 87-year-old event is likely to be a popular favourite for centuries to come.

The Giro d'Italia *winds through the Italian landscape.*

1903, many considered it unfeasible. After all, in 1899, a Tour de France automobile race was already thought a feat and the average speed of 30 miles per hour was considered impressive. But to tackle the same circuit on a bicycle! No one in those days, of course, ever could have imagined that a century later bicycle racers would loop around the country at nearly the same speeds as those early automobiles. Those crazy enough to sign up for the inaugural run were, well, a strange breed – a cross between circus *saltimbanques* and horse-racing jockeys. The analogy to equestrian sports does not simply come from the fact that participants wore brightly coloured, skin-tight outfits, but also because they spoke a mysterious, insider language specifically adapted to the intricacies of their sport. And, as in horse racing, the mystery often continued into the arena of competition, as unspoken arrangements between competitors were commonplace. In 1904, the Tour was almost abolished due to widespread cheating.

The first ever *Tour was part publicity stunt, part cannon-ball run.*

Participants in early Tours *resembled a cross between circus performers and horse-racing jockeys with their individual styles and racing antics.*

In difficult times, however, the circus spirit took over. Early Tour cyclists could be seen standing on their hands on chairs or demonstrating two-wheeled acrobatics. Of course, any of the 60 riders starting the 1903 Tour on a fixed-gear bike weighing in at more than 30 pounds (13.6 kg) had to be a little off his rocker. But history can thank them, especially the 21 who finished. They created the mould, one that included an unimaginable appetite for suffering and hard physical labour that remains the essence of any aspiring bicycle racer today.

From its early years *right up to the present day, the Tour de France has attracted cyclists with an insatiable appetite for suffering.*

Early in the Tour's *history riders rode for national teams and were responsible for the maintenance of their own equipment – hence the spare tyres twisted around their shoulders.*

THE MAKINGS OF
THE GREATEST RACE

In the early years, the race organizers concerned themselves with establishing their event and giving it lasting guidelines. Additional kilometres would be added (the race is now 3,350 kilometres – about 2,080 miles), not to mention the mythic mountains.

But while the first Tours represented spectacle as much as they did pure sport, organizers soon became increasingly interested in the competitive aspects of the event. As years went by, other events like the time trial and team time trial were added. Extra-curricular events such the ever-popular circus-like publicity caravan that rolls in front of the race also have been added to entertain spectators waiting for the race to pass. And in recent years, elements like the VIP start village have grown. But throughout the generations, race organizers have maintained that improving the sporting aspects of the race is the common denominator to any change. Current race director Jean-Marie Leblanc insists, 'It is our job to make the race even so that a climber has as much chance as a time trialler.'

With his comeback *from cancer, American Lance Armstrong (seen here in the 2001 race) has bolstered global interest in the Tour de France.*

**Tour director
Jean-Marie
Leblanc**

In an effort to connect all of France's major cities, the inaugural Tour was divided into six individual stages: Paris to Lyon, Lyon to Marseille, Marseille to Toulouse, Toulouse to Bordeaux, Bordeaux to Nantes, and Nantes to Paris. Stages averaged 250 miles (400 km) in length and were followed by several rest days. Riders tackled their first mountain, the modest Ballon d'Alsace, in 1905. But when the race ventured into the Pyrenees in 1910, riders called the race organizers 'assassins'. Forced to push and pedal their way up little more than cow paths, their cries were not unwarranted. But such hardships and the exploits that ensued soon became part of the Tour legend.

The Tour de France, *seen here in 1938, has always had an intensely romantic image with the general public.*

Riders *in earlier days of the Tour battled it out on the same demanding mountain passes as today's riders*

In 1969, competing for the first time, a rider named Eddy Merckx (see page 156) unveiled his immense strength when he waltzed away from his competitors on the famed Tourmalet climb in the Pyrenees, setting off on an epic 90-mile (145-km) solo ride that left his nearest competitor a full 8 minutes behind. 'What this sublime cyclist did,' wrote then-race-director Jacques Goddet, 'had never yet been written in the annals of the road.' In 1975, six years and five Tour victories later, the same Merckx, withered and worn by the years of intense racing, wilted on the climb to Pra-Loup in the Alps. It would be his last day in yellow.

(left) The Tour de France *passed through stunning Alpine scenery.*

(right) Merckx *had more stage wins and more days in yellow than any other Tour rider.*

In 1986, the legendary Alpe d'Huez was the stage for the historic transfer of power between two team-mates, five-time defending champion Bernard Hinault of France and his protégé, American Greg LeMond (see page 23). LeMond, in yellow, rode together with Hinault before handing his one-time master the stage victory. In 1991, Spaniard Miguel Indurain (see overleaf) forced LeMond's own defeat on the Val-Louron climb in the Pyrenees. But five years later Big Mig's own reign came to an end in the Alps when he faltered on the climb to Les Arcs.

Spain's Miguel Indurain was the first-ever rider to win five consecutive Tours de France.

Frenchman Bernard Hinault *had an iron grip on the Tour in the late '70s and early '80s. Today he is involved in organizing the race.*

MIGUEL INDURAIN
A Humble Hero

Amazed by his seemingly effortless string of stunning victories, his contemporaries deemed him 'the Alien', 'the Motorcycle' and 'Big Mig'. Though he was one of the most feared men in the pelotons of the 1990s, Miguel Indurain was defined as much by his humility and grace as his power and prowess.

A natural athlete, Indurain won the second road race he entered at the tender age of 12. He spent his teens tearing up the Spanish circuit and in 1985, aged 20, he joined his first professional team.

Victories proved more elusive as a pro, however, and Indurain spent five years as one of many strong, yet unremarkable European racers. Undaunted, he simply continued racing ... and improving, eventually winning a few prestigious races and capturing two Tour de France stage wins.

It all came together for Indurain in 1991, when he captured his first Tour de France victory. The following four years and five total consecutive Tour de France victories would establish Indurain as a legend of the sport, a label he graciously declined. 'You cannot compare me to them', he said of Eddy Merckx and Bernard Hinault. 'I just want to be Indurain.'

Today fans and fellow racers remember Indurain as much for the races he didn't win as for those he did. More than once, he ceded a sure win to a racer he deemed deserving of that day's top honours – a gentlemanly feat that will not soon be surpassed.

VITAL STATS

NATIONALITY: Spanish

DATE OF BIRTH: 16 July 1964

CAREER VICTORY HIGHLIGHTS: Tour de France: 1991, 1992, 1993, 1994, 1995; Giro d'Italia: 1992, 1993; Olympic Time Trial: 1992, 1993; World Cup Classic (*Clasica San Sebastián*): 1990

And, of course, American superhero Lance Armstrong has habitually used historic climbs such as Sestrières, Alpe d'Huez, or Hautacam to construct each of his five Tour victories. To date, none have defeated him.

Armstrong *has also written books about his life and his experiences as a cyclist.*

Certainly today, despite the century-old cries of 'assassin', the Tour is quite simply unthinkable without its legendary mountains. But Tour directors never limited their innovations to altitude. In an effort to add suspense, race organizers in the 1920s transformed flat stages into a sort of team time trial, where each team rode together, trying to post the best time. This formula, however, quickly proved flawed as it gave riders on strong teams an unfair advantage. In 1934, they introduced the first individual time trial, a 51.5-mile (83-km) timed stretch from La Roche-sur-Yon to Nantes. While it proved to be the undoing of race hero René Vietto, one of the race's first kings of the mountains, organizers considered it a success as it offered non-climbers a chance to make their mark. And today, time trialling is an integral part of every Tour.

(far left) Cycling *in a pack this close requires great skill and concentration.*

(left) Two burly riders *shake hands before the opening prologue of a 1934 time trial.*

The New Proving Ground

The third and final great three-week tour in Europe is the Vuelta a España, held each year in September, following the Giro d'Italia and the Tour de France. Though the Spanish tour is younger than the other two, not quite 60 years old, and somewhat less esteemed than the prized Italian and French events, the Vuelta is quickly becoming the race in which to catch cycling's newest rising stars.

Like the other major tours, the Vuelta alters its route slightly each year in an attempt to keep the race interesting and offer unique challenges to cyclists in every discipline. Climbers, in particular, can make their mark here, with legendary climbs such as El Angliru, a mountain so nearly vertical that racers say it makes other classic mountain passes feel like 'child's play' in comparison. Though Vuelta tends to be relatively short, spanning fewer than 2,000 miles (3,220 km), its numerous mountaintop finishes, time trials and sprinting stages make the Vuelta similar to the Tour de France in the mental and physical energy it takes to complete it. For that reason, up-and-coming pros use the

Vuelta to show off their form and attract media and sponsor attention. It is often said that if you can win the Vuelta, you're in the limelight for the Tour.

Even established pros have used the Vuelta as a proving ground. In 1999, German sensation Jan Ullrich dominated the Spanish tour as proof that after two years of problems and defeats, he was back in form. And in 1998, just two years after his stunning cancer disclosure, Lance Armstrong roared into the Vuelta, finishing in an impressive fourth place, as a sign that he could (and would) win the following year's Tour de France. The Vuelta may never get any bigger, but it certainly will not shrink in importance any time soon.

(left) Wearing the leader's jersey *in the Vuelta a España can be a precursor to Tour de France glory.*

(right) The route of the Vuelta *passes many of Spain's classic tourist destinations.*

THE MAGICAL MYSTERY OF THE TOUR

What makes the Tour so special is not simply its magnificent, truly unmatched sporting exploits, but also the relationship it has with its people. 'The Tour de France,' says current Tour director Leblanc, 'is an uncommon human adventure, an unequalled cycling race, but also an incredible popular and social event.'

The Tour de France succeeds in surpassing any other sporting event – the football World Cup and the Olympics included – for one simple reason: it takes sport outside the stadium. For three weeks every July, the small country roads of France become a non-stop stadium, lined with fans from around the world, who all manage to impose a certain carnival spirit on what remains a sporting event of the highest level. On these roads, fans commune with their heroes as racers often pass

within arm's length. It is not uncommon for fans to hand riders water bottles. Even an encouraging push to a lagging rider is overlooked. Race organizers ignore such details because they know that fans never push the better riders, for it is understood among the millions of fans that they should never affect the race between the favourites.

'France is a magical place for such a race,' says three-time winner Greg LeMond, ever popular in the land of the Tour. 'Everything comes together for the Tour. They close the country down for you. The roads take on their own identity. There is a romance to them and they belong to the Tour. You couldn't have this race in any other country.'

One of the busiest boulevards *in Paris, the Champs Elysées shuts down when the Tour comes to town.*

HEROES OF THE TOUR

(right) **Garin throws** *a glance over his shoulder to check the competition.*

In an almost uncanny fashion, each generation of Tour riders has produced their own breed of champion. From the carnivalesque Lucien Petit-Breton, winner of the Tour in 1907 and 1908, to the cannibalesque Eddy Merckx, winner of five Tours in the 1960s and 1970s, to the iron-like American Lance Armstrong, winner of the past five races – the great Tour champions all seem to somehow embody their age.

Appropriately for his time, the race's first champion, Maurice Garin, sported a handlebar moustache, which was fashionable in *fin-de-siècle* Europe and even more so for a bicycle racer. In 1908, the modest Petit-Breton became the first two-time winner of the Tour.

Maurice Garin (right) *stands behind his Tour-winning bike.*

Much of his notoriety, however, didn't come from the fact that he won the race twice, but that he rode as an independent on a makeshift bicycle, yet beat better-organized, more powerful riders and teams. His victories embodied the pioneering spirit of the Tour's first golden age.

In 1920, Belgium's Philippe Thys became the first three-time winner. Noted for his marathon training rides, his hard-work ethic gave hope to a generation recovering from the ruins of World War I.

Italian Gino Bartali *is one of the great characters to have won the Tour de France (in 1938 and 1948).*

Italy's Gino Bartali was similarly inspirational in 1948, when he won the Tour for a second time, 10 years after his first victory. Although he lost the golden years of his own career to World War II, his second victory showed the world that certain things could be as before.

He would be replaced in 1949 by his countryman Fausto Coppi, considered by many to be the first modern-day champion for his ability to incorporate a specialized diet and training to the sport.

Fausto Coppi *won the Tour de France twice and the hearts of his countrymen many times over with his indomitable spirit.*

JACQUES ANQUETIL
The Unconventional Champion

In a sport that prides itself on unwritten rules and codes of ethics, French sensation Jacques Anquetil was an aristocratic outlaw. From his unconventional style – toes pointed to the ground, arms and legs stretched like a spider – to his tactics – exert only enough to win – to his air of arrogance, 'Anq' was not a popular 'favourite'. Yet, his prowess during his 19-year reign was undeniable.

Anquetil rode himself into the top echelon of cycling dignitaries largely through his tremendous time-trialling abilities. He would simply hang close to his rivals for days on end, then blow them off the pavement on time-trial days – an approach that earned him five Tour de France victories. Though this measured strategy didn't win over fans, it did result in remarkable achievements. He was one of only two riders to win the Giro d'Italia and Tour de France in the same year. And in a seemingly superhuman feat, he won the 1965 Dauphiné Libéré, a gruelling week-long Alpine stage race, then flew to the western coast of France, slept four hours and rode off to victory in the rainy, dark 365-mile (588 km) Bordeaux–Paris race.

Ultimately, it wasn't his myriad podium finishes as much as his ability to suffer on the bike that earned Anquetil admirers. From smashing into a telephone pole at the completion of a wearisome, yet victorious, two-man time trial in 1962 to his talent for mashing enormous gears over monster climbs, Anquetil left little doubt of his unparalleled capabilities. Yet today, he remains one of the least appreciated champions of the sport.

VITAL STATS

NATIONALITY: French

DATE OF BIRTH: 8 January 1934

CAREER VICTORY HIGHLIGHTS: Tour de France: 1957, 1961, 1962, 1963, 1964; Giro d'Italia: 1960, 1964; Ghent–Wevelgem: 1964; Vuelta a España: 1963

Anquetil was the first rider *to win five Tours. Yet his unusual style and arrogant demeanour damaged his popularity with the public.*

Three-time winner Louison Bobet (1953, 1954, 1955) embodied the popular rebirth of the Tour after World War II, while his countryman Jacques Anquetil (see previous page), the race's first five-time winner (1957, 1961, 1962, 1963, 1964) was as famous for his playboy lifestyle in the swinging '60s as he was for his overwhelming exploits on the bike. Belgium's Eddy Merckx dominated the race in the late 1960s and early 1970s. While his long Elvis-like sideburns were perhaps slightly behind the times, he matched contemporary champions like Mohammad Ali with his insatiable appetite for winning, justifiably earning the nickname 'the Cannibal'.

France's Bernard Hinault brought the race back home by winning it five times between 1978 and 1985, but his successor, American Greg LeMond, symbolized the growing worldwide appeal of the race when he won it three times between 1986 and 1990.

In the years *after the Second World War, Louison Bobet was just the kind of hero France needed.*

Five-time winner Miguel Indurain reflected an age of increased specialization, focusing his energies only on the Tour during the late-1990s. And then, of course, there is today's dominant champion, Lance Armstrong (see page 207), who beat life-threatening cancer to become the top Tour rider of his generation. His ability to beat cancer as well as his ability to go on to compete are a triumph for modern medicine and technology. A meticulous champion with an insatiable appetite for suffering, Armstrong ignores no details in his training, diet or high-tech equipment.

(left) In the 1966 Tour *the motorcade follows the leader up into the Alps.*

(right) Like Hinault before him, *Armstrong is a master time-trial rider and tactician.*

But the Tour is as much about its many losers as it is about its celebrated winners. Eugène Christophe was the first rider to wear the famed yellow jersey when it was introduced midway through the 1919 race so that organizers and spectators could better discern the leader. Yet Christophe never won the race and lost two Tours in 1913 and 1919, when he broke his fork. In 1934, neophyte René Vietto won the public's heart but lost the Tour when he gave his front wheel to his team-mate Antonin Magne, the eventual winner. His generosity symbolized the team spirit in this originally individual sport. In the 1960s, Raymond Poulidor continually came up short in the face of iron-man Jacques Anquetil and in the 1970s, he fell behind Eddy Merckx. While 'Pou Pou' never wore the yellow jersey for a single day, he always seemed to win the popularity contest.

Although he never won the Tour or even wore the leader's jersey, Poulidor is still loved as a champion in France.

A Time-Honoured Tradition

Peek below the surface of any rough and tumble professional peloton and you'll notice a strangely soft underside – shaved legs. Though shearing one's legs baby-bottom smooth has long been considered decidedly feminine, cyclists worldwide have adopted the practice as a symbol of a rider's commitment to the sport.

No one's really sure where the tradition got started, or why, but there's plenty of speculation. Better aerodynamics is one of the most common explanations. But even the most hard-core cyclists freely admit that the 1,000th of a second that they save on wind resistance is hardly a deciding factor. More logical are the claims that shaved legs are easier to clean and they heal more quickly after a crash. Since many cyclists also frequent massage therapists to soothe their muscles and speed recovery, having smooth, hairless

quadriceps and calves allows for a more fluid rubdown, free of painful, awkward hair yanking.

Then there's the vanity factor. Reasonable explanations aside, some cyclists will admit they shave their legs simply because it makes them look better. Pushing pedals over hundreds of miles creates diamond-cut calves and bulging quads. As any body builder will tell you, those muscles are easier

to admire without a mass of hair in the way. This could explain why some cyclists shave year-round though they may not be anywhere near a bike during the cold winter months.

You certainly don't need to shave your legs to be considered a dedicated cyclist, but if you see a well-muscled man with fuzz-barren legs, you can safely guess he's a member of the club.

Smoothly shaved legs, *one of the great traditions in professional cycling.*

THE DARK SIDE OF THE TOUR

Sponsorship logos
*dominate the scene as
Miguel Indurain and
Claudio Chiappucci
ascend an alpine pass.*

The mass popularity of the Tour has not come without a price. Since the race's inception, the inherent charm of the Tour has been marred by hype and scandal. Director Leblanc often laments that 'the Tour is a victim of its own success' – a claim that is not unwarranted.

Business and marketing interests continue to take the spotlight off of the racing, focusing instead on the show *around* the race. The famed publicity caravan continually lengthens; the marketing and consumer side of the event seemingly never ceases to grow. Today the number of official race vehicles commands disproportionate significance, making it increasingly difficult for spectators to actually see the race. And many journalists, who traditionally followed the race so they could add colourful details to their reports, simply prefer to watch on

With multi-national giants *like Coca-Cola putting their name on the line, the Tour is big business.*

television from the press hall rather than fight with VIP cars for a glimpse of the race.

And then there is the infamous 'D' word. Drugs are the most nagging problem. Since bicycle racing's pioneer years, the sport (with the Tour as its most high-profile event) has been prey to accusations of drugs. And, as witnessed in the notorious Festina Affair in 1998, cycling has never been able to free itself from such sinister vices. As early as 1908, after his second Tour victory, Petit-Breton defended himself against drugging charges in the pages of *L'Auto*, the race's sponsoring newspaper: 'It's been said that I owe my principal victories to drugs. Permit me to deny this absurd noise.'

But over the years there have been too many proven cases of doping to discount the issue simply as 'absurd noise'. In 1924, the legendary Pelissier brothers abandoned the race over what they considered to be an unfair ruling. Later that day, they met with journalist Albert Londres in a roadside bar. 'You don't have any idea of what the Tour is,' said an obviously frustrated Henri. 'We suffer from beginning to end. You want to see how we ride? Look. Here is the cocaine for the eyes. Here is the chloroform for the gums. And the pills? You want to see the pills?' After reaching in his sack and grabbing an assortment of pills, his brother Francis added, 'In short, we ride on dynamite.'

Festina team leader, *Frenchman Richard Virenque was at the centre of the 1998 scandal that endangered the existence of the Tour.*

JAN ULLRICH
A Troubled Champion

In 1996, at only 22, Jan Ullrich took second place in the Tour de France and a year later he swept home to win. A notoriously powerful climber and time triallist, the cycling world was at his feet – until the ground beneath them began to crumble.

Ullrich started racing at the tender age of 8, and by 13 was being groomed for a professional career. His youthful dedication paid off when powerhouse team Telekom signed him in 1995. After his Tour de France success in 1997. Ullrich became a superstar. Too much celebration and too little training, however, left him about 25 pounds (11.35 kg) overweight for the 1998 Tour, which he lost to Marco Pantani. A knee injury cut his 1999 season short. Alhough he scored victories in the Olympics and the World Championships in the following seasons, he rolled into the 2000 Tour overweight and lost to Lance Armstrong, who beat him again in 2001.

In 2002, a frustrated Ullrich came apart at the seams. Chronic knee problems again forced him from the Tour. Shortly thereafter, he crashed his car in a drink-driving incident and was later suspended for six months after testing positive for drugs he took at a club.

2003 began positively with a strong performance against Armstrong in what would become one of the closest races for many years. But with a crash on the slippery roads during the time trial from Pornic to Nantes, Ullrich lost his momentum, and with it his chances of eroding Armstrong's one-minute lead. Once again, Ullrich finished the Tour in second place.

Ullrich's next opportunity to win the Tour will be 2004: time will tell if the the star is indeed rising again.

VITAL STATS

NATIONALITY: German

DATE OF BIRTH: 2 December 1973

CAREER VICTORY HIGHLIGHTS: Tour de France: 1997; Vuelta a España: 1999; Olympic Road: 2000; German Road Championship: 2001; World Championships Time Trial: 2001

In 1960, French up-and-comer Roger Rivière crashed on a descent in the Pyrenees and was paralysed for life. Amphetamines were found in his jersey pocket. British rider Tom Simpson collapsed and died on Mont Ventoux in the 1967 Tour. Similar substances were found in his body.

And today, even with the rise of sports science that should eliminate the need for doping, the temptation is often too great. Unfortunately, the Festina Affair was likely an indication of a greater problem. Less than a year later, Italy's Marco Pantani, winner of the 1998 Tour, was expelled while leading the Giro d'Italia when he failed to pass a blood test. Numerous other cases of doping within the sport continue to compromise the efforts of those riders who are clean. And because the Tour is cycling's flagship event, it suffers indirectly from any doping scandal reported within the sport.

Despite such flaws, the Tour – justifiably considered a French national landmark – continues to grow in popularity. Perhaps no century could have been better than the 20th to cradle such a competition. It will be remembered as a century of great innovation when man continually pushed the boundaries of his own limitations. And in no other sporting event have athletes continually pushed their own physical and psychological limits day in and day out.

British rider Tom Simpson *collapsed near the summit of Mont Ventoux during the 1967 Tour. Today a monument marks the spot where he died.*

Although the event becomes increasingly high-tech and the media and marketing hype continue to snowball, there remains a timeless element to the Tour, a simple bike race rolling across the magnificent landscape of France. There is a simple beauty to this event that defies civilization's eternal march toward modernity. It is this endearing aspect of the world's greatest bike race that continues to capture our imagination. Perhaps that is why every man, woman and child who has seen this race, even for a passing instant, remembers it for a lifetime.

Despite the forces *pulling at the* Grande Boucle, *its beauty and drama is timeless.*

AFTERWORD

By Joe Lindsey

The trail beckons, crookedly. It drops away beneath you, picking a delicate path among rocks and roots, twisting around trees and grade reversals, before disappearing gradually into the trees. Your front wheel rolls into the first section; the line appears unbidden before you and the bike floats over, rather than through, the rock garden. Your unblinking eyes scan farther down the trail, mentally picking up and storing each section and the means to get through it in your short-term subconscious. Your brain is active, taking in a thousand myriad interpretations and options to plot the right solution but is at the same time perfectly calm, unobstructed by extraneous thought; consciousness only momentarily surfaces amid the bliss of simply riding.

These emotions and experiences transform us, not just as cyclists, but as people. In our everyday lives, cycling helps us in ways we cannot count. We are fitter, healthier people. Riding is a demanding sport, one that opens up a world of healthier habits and lifestyle, of eating well and of the benefits of exercise. The determination to stick out the last few miles of a century when you're dehydrated and sore, muscles cramping, transfers almost seamlessly to other aspects of life. Any challenge becomes easier to meet because you have faced and overcome obstacles on the bike.

The act of riding is also solace, meditation. It calms and adds clarity, perspective to the ability to deal with problems. A ride is a mental reset button, a ritual we undertake when we need time for ourselves, time spent doing something purely for the joy of it, in search of the moment when we lose our names and our identities and become simply the act of riding.

When you experience that perfect moment, your heart must sink because you know you can never find it again – it has come and passed and cannot be held on to or even properly remembered; memory would require your conscious self to be present, and it wasn't. But you must still try; you must search for that feeling again and again. It is what it means to ride.

The sensations riding evokes in us – the exhilarating rush of speed that gives us wings, the rawness of morning air drawn into the lungs, the sense of losing self in self – these are all the reasons we ride. We ride because it feels like flying. We ride because it feels like home.

ILLUSTRATION CREDITS

Cover (front & back)

Photograph by Mitch Mandel/Rodale Images; the bicycle is a 1952 Schwinn American (Serial No. F224154, manufactured in Chicago c. 31 October 1952).

Interior

© The Bicycle Museum of America: pages 5, 132 (safety bike, Schwinn Excelsior), 148 (chain drive bike), 154

© Jeremy Rendell/Taxi/Getty Images: page 6

© AFP/Corbis: pages 9, 11, 13, 74, 77, 83, 124, 135, 210, 235, 276 (Le Blanc), 278, 284, 286 (Vuelta a España), 287 (Vuelta a España), 292 (Garin), 303 (bike team), 306, 307 (Ullrich)

© Lonny Kalfus/Stone/Getty Images: page 14

© PhotoDisc: pages 16 (kids), 22 (kids), 36 (kids)

© John Kelly/The Image Bank/Getty Images: page 16 (family)

© Erik Rank/Photonica: pages 16 (shadow), 22 (shadow), 36 (shadow)

© H. Armstrong Roberts/Corbis: page 17

© Bilderberg/Photonica: page 18 (background)

© Hulton Archive: pages 18 (Beckett), 23 (background), 25, 30 (Einstein), 34, 36 (bike accident), 38, 39, 43, 44, 45 (boys), 48, 49, 63 (background), 67, 70 (background), 71 (background), 93 (background), 97, 100, 111, 116 (background), 120, 122 (large-wheel tricycle), 123, 126, 132 (large-wheel tricycle, velocipede, high wheeler, recumbent), 133 (Spacelander), 136 (large-wheel tricycle), 137, 141, 142, 145, 146, 147, 151, 152 (tire), 153, 156, 157 (background), 158 (large-wheel tricycle), 159, 162 (large-wheel tricycle), 168 (background), 169 (background), 180, 181 (man), 183, 187 (da Vinci), 207 (background), 230 (background), 231 (background), 248 (background), 276 (Tour de France), 279, 282 (background), 296 (background), 297 (background), 307 (background)

© Doug Plummer/Photonica: page 19

© Mel Curtis/Photonica: page 20

© Lego/Taxi/Getty Images: page 22 (bike with training wheels)

© Photosport International: pages 23 (LeMond), 30 (background), 31 (background), 50 (background), 51 (background), 66 (background), 69 (background), 87 (background), 90 (background), 91 (background), 108 (background), 116 (Coppi), 130 (background), 134 (background), 135 (background), 157 (Merckx), 165 (background), 172 (background), 173 (background), 187 (background), 194 (background), 201 (background), 219 (background), 234 (Lassalle), 236 (background), 237 (background), 254 (background), 264, 266, 268 (background), 269 (background), 271, 272, 273, 274, 280, 283, 286 (background), 287 (background), 288 (Coppi, Hinault), 290, 292 (Coppi, Hinault), 293, 294, 295, 296 (Anquetil), 297 (Anquetil), 299, 300, 302, 303 (background), 304 (Coppi, Hinault), 305, 309

© Steve Niedorf Photography/The Image Bank/Getty Images: page 24

© Bettmann/Corbis: pages 26, 62, 64, 115, 128, 129, 132 (swiftwalker), 143, 144, 182, 184, 204 (women), 205 (couple, Katharine Hepburn, performer)

© Karen Cipolla/Photonica: page 27

© Gerd George/Taxi/Getty Images: page 28

© California Institute of Technology: page 31 (Einstein)

© Charles Gullung/Photonica: page 32

© BikeFix: page 33

© Harold Sinclair/Photonica: page 37

© John Terence Turner/Taxi/Getty Images: page 40

© Johner/Photonica: page 41

© Luc Beziat/Stone/Getty Images: page 42

© Brian Bailey/Stone/Getty Images: pages 45 (adult & child), 259

© Werran/Ochsner/Photonica: page 46

© The Des Moines Register: page 50 (Karras, RAGBRAI)

© Steven Puetzer/Photonica: page 52

© Arthur Tress/Photonica: page 54

© Corbis: pages 56, 58 (BMX biker), 60 (BMX biker), 82 (BMX biker), 94 (BMX biker), 102 (BMX biker), 106 (BMX biker), 117 (BMX biker), 133 (BMX biker), 140, 148 (boneshaker), 178 (bicycle), 188, 190, 192 (bicycle), 197, 198 (portrait), 202, 203, 204 (bicycle, woman), 205 (muscleman), 208 (bicycle), 244, 320

© Brad Whol/American Cyclery: pages 58 (mural), 60 (mural), 82 (mural), 94 (mural), 102 (mural), 106 (mural), 117 (mural)

© Ken Reid/Taxi/Getty Images: page 59

© AP Photo/Laurent Rebours: page 61

Courtesy of the Major Taylor Association and *The Extraordinary Career of a Champion Bicycle Racer Major Taylor:* page 63

© Hulton-Deutsch Collection/Corbis: pages 66 (racers), 114, 131, 150, 158 (biker), 285

© Mike King/Corbis: page 68

© 1997 Donna H. Chiarelli/Lehigh Valley Velodrome: page 69 (velodrome)

© Pavlovsky Jacques/Corbis Sygma: page 70 (bike)

© Reuters NewMedia Inc./Corbis: pages 71 (Boardman), 72, 112, 113, 262, 269 (Giro d'Italia), 281, 289, 301, 304 (bike team), 310

© AP Photo/Peter Dejong: page 75

© AP Photo/Matt York: page 78

© 1996 Tom Moran: page 80

© Duomo/Corbis: pages 81, 92, 93 (Mirra), 207 (Armstrong)

ABOUT THE CONTRIBUTORS

Bill Strickland is an executive editor of *Bicycling* magazine. He has ridden and written about the sport of cycling for more than 20 years; raced on the road, on mountain bikes, and in velodromes; published stories in *Men's Health, Men's Journal, Blue, Parenting* and other US magazines; and commented on cycling for TV programmes such as *Good Morning America* and *The Early Show*. His books include *The Quotable Cyclist, Mountain Biking: The Ultimate Guide to the Ultimate Ride,* and *On Being a Writer.*

Mark Riedy fell in love with cycling at the age of 13. Since then he's lived and ridden in New York, Los Angeles and San Francisco. He's written and worked for *Bicycling* and *Mountain Bike* magazines for nearly a decade and has contributed to *Outside, Popular Science,* and *I.D.* magazines as well as books on cycling and other subjects.

Joe Lindsey has raced and ridden bikes for 15 years and is a contributing writer to *Bicycling* magazine. His work has also appeared in *Outside, Adventure Sports* and *5280* magazines, and he has contributed to several of Fodor's travel guides. He has written about cycling since graduating from the University of Colorado eight years ago, covering the people, places, events and culture that make the sport such a fascinating activity.

Nicholas Oddy is a bicycle historian and lecturer in the History of Design in the historical and critical studies department at Glasgow School of Art. He has presented various talks on the bicycle, most notably 'An Invaluable Refinement: The Aesthetic of the Cycle Accessory in the Late 19th and 20th Centuries' at the 1996 International Cycle History Conference held in Buffalo.

Zapata 'Zap' Espinoza has worked for *LA Weekly* and *Motocross Action* magazines and as an editor of *Mountain Bike Action* magazine, which under his leadership became the largest mountain bike publication in the industry. He's spent recent years writing for *Bicycling* and *Mountain Bike* magazines. Espinoza is one of the most visible and colourful figures in mountain-bike journalism.

James Startt, admittedly nothing more than pack fodder in the 1992 Olympic trials, has made his greatest contribution to the sport as a journalist and a photographer. Now an avid lunchtime cyclist, Startt, the European correspondent to *Bicyling*, has covered 14 Tours de France and is the author of *Tour de France/Tour de Force*, the first history of the Tour de France written in English.

Additional material from **Selene Yeager**, a certified fitness trainer, avid cyclist, expert-class mountain-bike racer, triathlete, professional writer, and author of *Selene Yeager's Perfectly Fit*. She is a contributing editor at *Prevention* magazine and writes on training programmes in *Bicycling* magazine. Her work has also appeared in *Men's Health, Runner's World, Cosmopolitan, Fitness* and *Marie Claire* magazines.

INDEX